OUTPOSTS
OF LOVE

D1508740

By Maria Anne Hirschmann

Maria Anne Hirschmann

OUTPOSTS OF LOVE

Fleming H. Revell Company
Old Tappan, New Jersey

Library of Congress Cataloging in Publication Data

Hirschmann, Maria Anne.
    Outposts of love.

    1. Missions, American. 2. Hirschmann, Maria Anne.
I. Title.
BV2410.H54   266'.023'095   76-45401
ISBN 0-8007-0839-3

Contents

INTRODUCTION:
Meet the *True American*

I had heard about the *ugly American* years before meeting my first American in person. Nazi propaganda brainwashed me into picturing American men as revolver-carrying, gum-chewing gangsters and America as a land where a few rich capitalists exploited the masses in sweatshops and on cotton plantations.

I had no reason not to believe what the Nazis told me. Yet I sometimes remembered that during my childhood years—before being chosen to be specially educated in a Nazi school—I had heard some of the villagers saying the word *America* with nearly the same reverence as the word *God.* They had relatives who had emigrated across the great waters and made their *Glück* (good fortune and luck).

Shortly after World War I my own foster parents had accepted the doctrines of a church that originated in America, and I remembered my mother's eyes filling with awe as she spoke of that land. We obtained a few doctrinal books written in American and translated into German, and although they were yellow with age, they became Mother's great inspiration and joy outranked only by the Bible. Year after year Mother read and reread those books from America.

When Hitler conquered Czechoslovakia, my homeland, certain words disappeared from our daily vocabulary. America was one of those words. By the time it came back to my attention, that word had acquired a new, ugly sound, and I had learned to detest it.

By the end of World War II, I not only hated the word, I hated Americans, although I had never seen one except in Nazi war movies. I hated them because they had come across the ocean to fight us Germans "for no good reason." I hated them as enemies in their own right and as allies of the Russian troops who occupied our territory and treated us cruelly after they defeated us. Even when I decided to flee to the American Military Zone of Western Germany to escape the Communists, I knew that I would never want to cross paths with any Americans.

Fate seemed against me. The very first person I encountered after finally slipping past the last Russian rifle and the East German border-line was an American soldier. He looked just as I expected him to. He carried a revolver and chewed gum. But he didn't *do* what I expected. In fact, he did what I expected least. He smiled. He invited me and my two fellow refugee girls into his GI barracks, and there, to my astonishment, those "American enemies" fed us, offered us for our rest a private room with cots and blankets, and at last they let us go! Waving and smiling after us, they actually let us walk away unmolested with no strings attached to their kindness. It was incredible!

I'll never forget the confusion I felt at that moment when we three girls walked away from that odd building and those young, cheering Americans. Physically I felt rested. My stomach bulged for the first time in long months, but my head spun in bewilderment. I had expected struggle, cruelty, rape, or death—things I had been forced to expect ever since Russian soldiers had stepped into my daily life. Instead, I received help, warmth, smiles, and jokes, and I didn't understand why. Why were these allies of the Russians different? Were all of them like that? Was there more than one kind of American? Who were these young men anyway, and what made them do what they did? Had I been taught wrong in Nazi school?

I wondered about it for a long time. Nearly ten years after I had met my first Americans, I began to find some answers. In 1955 my family and I immigrated from West Germany to the United States. The first year after our arrival seemed only to deepen my confusion. Culture shock and homesickness overwhelmed me too much to seek any answers but survival. Little by little my family and I began to adapt to the American way of life. I began to look around and wonder again: Who were the Americans anyway? Were they really different? Were there many kinds? If so, why?

Meeting more and more of them, I decided that Americans *are* unique, diverse, and sometimes hard for people of another culture to understand. Also there are many kinds of Americans. Like their land, they come in various forms, shapes, and dispositions. America includes big wide plains, stately mountains, dry deserts, never-melting glaciers, endless snow, and everlasting summer sun. Some soil produces abundantly year after year; other places yield food or shelter reluctantly. The American continent is a land of many and sharp contrasts—and so are its people.

I found that a few, a small percentage of Americans, are as ugly as I once thought them all to be. Gun-carrying gangsters exist not only in many Hollywood movies but in the streets of our cities. There are ugly Americans who exploit their fellowmen in our own and in other countries. I was aware of that long before I read the best seller *The Ugly American*, and I didn't question the story when I finally read it. I even granted the two authors the right to claim their message as truth although it was put into a fictional setting. But it puzzled me that so many American people seemed to be so proud of that book and its title. Why? Why did they buy so many copies? Why would American lecturers quote from it with crisp sarcasm and a certain satisfaction in their voices? The book made me bristle in defense of my new homeland and the millions of Americans who *never* were ugly, greedy, or bad, either in the past or now. I had found the majority of the Americans to be helpful, kind, tolerant—and very naive.

I couldn't help but love them although I haven't completely learned to understand some of their strange habits yet. After twenty-one years of living in the USA and becoming an American citizen, I still have a few puzzling questions left: Why do Americans have such an obsession to put themselves and their native homeland down? Why do books, films, newspapers, and the news media display the ugly profile of a few Americans—even to the extent of glorification—but nobody ever speaks about the real, the true, the beautiful American? What will that negative trend do to our youth—to my own five children, who are Americans by choice or birth?

Nobody can deny that negatives *do* exist. Watergate has happened. There *are* Americans who don't believe in the law and love and the fundamentals of our nation any more. But for every ugly American I ever met, I have found a true one—or two—or ten or a hundred.

I have found him *in* America as my neighbor who lives next door to me. I have found him abroad, all around the globe, on my world tour: preaching, teaching, helping, healing, giving of himself to the end. Nobody ever speaks about him, for what he is doing does not make eye-catching headlines or book thrillers. Love and helping are too common to the American way of life to be acknowledged as an extraordinary thing.

I feel that it is high time for someone to tell the *other* side of *The Ugly American*. May I have the privilege of doing so? May the former Nazi girl, who once hated America without knowing better, tell you what she has seen and heard on her last world tour (December 1974 to January 1975)?

The true American is alive and in action everywhere—at home and overseas. He keeps America from falling apart and brings about the blessings that God bestows on our country even today. It is time that someone speak up for him! It is time to meet him or her.

America, will you stand up and proudly salute your sons and daughters? Will you at least read and listen?

> Your fellow American,
> HANSI

OUTPOSTS OF LOVE

1
Takeoff

How is it possible that something so ugly, dirty, and gray as Los Angeles smog can turn into pure liquid gold and heavenly splendor at certain sunsets? The California sky was ablaze with fire and crimson clouds as our jet rose high toward the west. What a way to begin a world trip!

Too bad my spirit didn't match the grandeur of the sky. I had a hard time showing enthusiasm at all. I simply was too tired to enjoy anything but sleep. Of course, it wasn't right to sleep on my first trip to Hawaii; after all, I had dreamed about going there for many years and had pictured it in vivid colors. Here I sat by a window and tried to force myself to feel excited and to imprint on my memory that great anticipated moment. All I could do was yawn!

My day had been planned very carefully. I was to speak for a women's luncheon, and after that there would be ample time to slip into a pantsuit for the trip and get to the airport on time—so we thought! American audiences are precious—and very perturbed if a speaker does not have all the time in the world at the end of her speech to visit, shake hands, autograph books, and listen patiently to what people, especially women, like to say.

By the time I had autographed, listened, smiled, and cried with all the ladies who wanted to see me, time had flown by and I rushed to change, rushed to say more good-byes, and rushed to the airport. That's where the rush ended. We crawled during rush-hour traffic. The most nerve-racking part of any trip is the car ride to the airport, at least in some places. People often spend more hours getting there than being in the air. However, the flight to Hawaii proved long enough to give me several hours of sleep, and I felt better when I arrived in Honolulu.

Hawaii is a foretaste of the Orient but with enough United States mixed into it to ease the shock to the American mind.

Where else but in Hawaii can one draw in the strong scent of exotic flowers and the bright colors of the Oriental market while kicking leisurely some empty aluminum soft drink cans that litter the sidewalks in typical American fashion? The Hawaiian sky is as blue or bluer than California sky, and there is just one thing different. Raindrops fall out of it ever so often, and rainbows seem to hold the different green islands together. It's beautiful but very devastating to hairdos for people who like to walk!

Nobody should plan to stay only one day in Hawaii, but it is better than going straight from the United States to the Orient. Without a day's stop, the time change can be hard on one's inner time clock. The flight from Honolulu to Japan is long enough, but from the West Coast of the USA it can be more than wearisome.

Our travel group assembled in Hawaii, some arriving only hours before we started out again. There were seven of us at first; in Korea we were joined by Cathy, a black gospel singer. Our group proved to be typically American in composition. There were Olin and Doris, who both had previously lost their mates of many years, now freshly married and on their honeymoon. Bill and Virginia were a retired couple who had toured the world before, except for Africa. Jim, the Midwest leader of a well-known American service and childcare organization, was our experienced guide. He had gone around the world several times, and he was obviously an old pro. Ann, my associate and personal friend, had the overwhelming task of looking after me.

Seven strangers set out together to visit faraway places—eight people came back, tied together forever by unbreakable bonds of friendship and common concerns.

2
Korea

The icy wind took me by surprise and so did the armed soldiers with cocked carbines and stony faces at every door. The security was unbelievably tight, and every Japanese passenger especially was checked with greatest suspicion. The contrast of the light atmosphere of the Japanese airline full of American Christmas music and the pasted-on smiles of their pretty stewardesses with the austere reception at the Seoul airport was overwhelming. I woke up to something I had almost forgotten: Some countries live with war the way America lives with peace. It's a way of life and people get used to it, on both sides. I found out later why the security was so tight the day we arrived. The Korean president's wife had been murdered just days before by a Japanese man.

Our spirits lifted a bit after we finally got through customs and were received by a delegation of Koreans, Americans, and an armful of red carnations. Harriet, a motherly American woman with white hair and a warm smile, made me feel better the moment we shook hands.

"Welcome to Korea," she said. "It isn't as cold every day as it is today!"

Later I was told that South Koreans claim that they have a "mild" winter that is occasionally interrupted by three successive cold days. They claim that only the Communist North has the bitterly cold Siberian-type winter! I have no idea what happened while we were in South Korea, but I couldn't find too much "mild" winter to keep me from freezing through a whole week.

Energy crisis is more than a debate in Korea; it is real. The price of fuel and gasoline is sky high. The poor suffer while the well-to-do put up with inconveniences. That came home to me when I walked into the

Chosun Hotel for a hair appointment. My hair had needed attention ever since the Hawaiian rain had caught me unawares. I tried hard to revive my looks before speaking to an International Women's Club in that fancy place for a luncheon.

The Chosun Hotel is perhaps the biggest and most elaborate place of its kind in Seoul. Plush red velvet, crystal chandeliers, thick Oriental rugs, hand-carved wood, and walls with flourished gold lines around tapestry and Oriental art reminded me in some ways of the royal palaces in Europe. I expected the prices in the elegant shops and the restaurants to be royal, too, but I was surprised! It was in reach of my limited budget. Even the price of the hairdresser was pleasant but not the water they washed my hair with. It was ice cold, and nobody bothered to apologize for it. So I acted as if it didn't bother me either, and we parted with a smile and many bows. Cold water to wash the hair or anything else is the least of the Koreans' concerns. They have harsher things to worry about.

Korea is just about the size of Great Britain or the state of New York. The South and North are divided at the thirty-eighth parallel, which leaves South Korea slightly smaller than the North but more heavily populated. Before I knew the statistical density of the population I had it already figured out that Korea, just like Japan, has wall-to-wall people. I wasn't surprised to find out that this tiny land ranks fourth in population density in the world.

What that does to the Seoul traffic and other related problems cannot be described; it has to be experienced. Nearly 6 million (out of the 32 million South Koreans) live and move in Seoul. Not everybody can afford a car; the working class gets around by buses or taxis. Seoul is called the city of 20,000 taxis! I thought I knew everything about heavy traffic because I get caught ever so often in Los Angeles rush hour traffic, but Los Angeles freeways are child's play compared to Oriental traffic.

The good Lord saw to it that we got used to it by degrees. We didn't make use of taxis or city buses while in Seoul. We were the guests of the American organization Jim belonged to, and they provided a small bus and chauffeur for us. It seemed bad enough for a start. I wasn't the only one who would ever so often shut both eyes tight as we watched Bill, our Korean driver, dive into ceaseless traffic from a side street. Every time he would emerge miraculously and without a scratch on the other side to plunge anew into the midst of a confused, honking mass of taxis, overloaded buses, motorcycles, and bicycles that seemed to move without apparent traffic rules.

It took me a few days to notice that we hardly ever saw accidents or drivers angry at each other. Those people had an almost stoic imperturbability and tolerance toward each other and their crowded way of life. To picture the same unmethodical hubbub in any United States city made me shudder. The American drivers would curse and murder each other with more than honking horns and threatening fists, at least for a while. Perhaps some day by future necessity Americans might learn Oriental patience, too—the Western world is getting more crowded every year, also!

The Orientals have one advantage when it comes to limited life space. They are as a race smaller and shorter than the average American. I was told that Koreans are generally taller and more robust than most Orientals. Nevertheless, they were still much shorter than anyone of our group, including Ann who is a whole five feet tall. Ann had to get used to looking down into people's eyes; she usually looks up to everyone.

Koreans may be short in stature, but they are a strong and persevering people, tough and tenacious like their bare, windswept land.

"I can't believe what I see," Jim said to me. "The recovery from war, destruction, and hunger is startling. Those Koreans have come back from nothing within a few years."

I had not seen Korea as Jim did right after the Korean War, but I had a pretty good idea what it must have been. Germany was in a similar chaos just a few years before the Communists tore into South Korea.

Yes, the Korean people had picked up the shattered pieces of their land and lives, and I could feel for them. They were patiently working toward a better and newer future. The traces of their courage and hard work were everywhere—and so were the footprints of another people: the compassionate Americans.

I picked up that track clearly among the hundreds of new impressions the very first day we arrived and long before the Korean War history and political structure came into focus for me. I had only very dim recollections about anything connected with the Korean War because we lived in postwar Germany during those years and paid not much attention to anything but our own refugee needs.

I'll never forget when we were taken right from the Seoul airport to the headquarters of Jim's organization for lunch and briefing. The brick building stood on a hill, and the place swarmed with children and adults.

"These are some of our orphans," Harriet smiled. "You'll have time later to meet them. Let's go and eat first!"

A strange smell hit my nostrils as we entered the dining area. I had never in my life smelled anything like it. I detected some fishy odor mixed with something sour or fermented similar to sauerkraut.

We sat down and said grace while I looked with a sorry smile at Ann. She has a very sensitive stomach, and I wasn't sure that she would find enough that her stomach would be able to tolerate. We had barley tea, fish soup, seaweed, and fried fish cakes besides big bowls of white rice, but the main dish was *kimchi,* a peppery, fermented cabbage that Koreans store underground in earthen jars all through the winter. Rice, soup, and *kimchi* are the basic simple diet of everyday Korean meals; for visitors fancy foods like our fried fish cakes are prepared with much effort and labor. I considered myself lucky that I like fish so much. I ate some of everything (including *kimchi*) while poor Ann displayed a sudden appetite for plain white rice and barley tea.

The Koreans who served us seemed to be genuinely pleased to welcome us Americans with everything they had to offer. Their love and respect were obvious. Americans are considered very special and are deeply admired by the South Korean people. I noticed that fact from the very first contact to the last moment I spent in Korea, and it didn't take me long to find out why.

"Who started this place?" I asked while we ate and talked.

I was told that it all started with a young American named Bob, who came in 1950 as a UN war correspondent to Korea. His heart was already broken by the sight of the suffering he had previously seen in China. He told of an incident that happened while he was in China. He visited a place where an American missionary woman from Michigan tried to keep hungry children alive. The woman was already sharing her own noontime bowl of rice with six children, but there was another girl, Tan, who followed the woman everywhere. The missionary looked at Bob and said, "I can't share my food with another or no one will have enough to live. I tell this one to go away while we eat! . . ." Tears filled the woman's eyes, and she picked up the scrawny child and almost threw her into Bob's arms.

"What are *you* going to do about her?" she asked.

Bob held that frail child and thought of his own two children back home. He handed the woman all the money he had and pledged to send more. He kept his pledge. Tan was fed until the Communists took over.

Bob saw thousands of hungry Tans and Kims and Chongs in Korea, too—and he decided to *do* something about it. No, he had no money, but he had something else: faith in God and his fellow Americans.

He came back to the United States and went on radio and television, he wrote articles and gave speeches, and hundreds of thousands of Americans responded—why?

Because the true American would rather help than hurt—because so many Americans believe in love.

3

Orphans, Candles, and Church Bells

Anything special or worthwhile starts with a dream in someone's mind. Invisible dreams are the foundation of visible things. Twenty-five years ago a young American named Bob cared enough to dream big, and I looked into the shiny eyes of hundreds of orphans who are alive today because of him.

Have you ever looked into the eyes of an orphan—any orphan? They all seem to have a special hunger in their eyes. It's a hunger for love, belonging, to be held, to be special to somebody. I know that hunger. I lived with it myself through all my childhood.

Ever since I was a little girl I dreamed about having an orphanage someday. I would brighten many of my lonely, drab childhood hours by thinking about it. My imaginary rooms were decorated and were named after all my favorite flowers. The windows had frilly curtains, and the soft beds had dolls and teddy bears on the pillows for the orphans to sleep with—all things I never had. My childish dreams have matured, of course, but I was little prepared for the stark contrast of my dream orphanage with what I saw in the many orphanages I visited in Korea and other countries of the world. Orphanages in the Orient are buildings with many empty rooms—rooms without any furniture, which permits large groups of orphans to occupy every bit of space.

"Where do the children sleep?" I asked aghast, when I stepped into that first orphanage in Korea.

"On the floor," a smiling native answered. She seemed to be amused by my consternation.

"On the cold, hard floor, without a mattress?" I curled my freezing toes up. The floor felt ice-cold. (In Korea shoes are taken off before entering any house.)

"Oh," the director of the orphanage assured me, "don't worry, the children have nice quilts to cover themselves!"

He pointed toward a neatly folded pile of quilts and stroked the top of them.

"Look, they are soft and warm. They were sent to us from America. Our children here have it better than many others in Korea. They have a solid roof over their heads, a quilt, and enough rice to eat!"

He looked at my wiggling toes.

"I know," he said, "the floors are cold. Normally these floors are warm —Koreans heat their houses through a simple heating system below the floor. Owing to the energy crisis we are not able to do it well enough this winter."

He smiled and bowed.

"We apologize that your feet must suffer on our cold floors!"

I shook my head. Never mind my cold feet, I thought. I will leave within a week to go to a country with a hot climate. I also carry in my pocket a ticket and a passport that give me, at the end of my trip, the beautiful privilege to go back home again—home to America. There I have a home with a carpeted warm floor and a hundred other luxuries these children do not even know or dream of.

They didn't seem to miss it, though, they were so excited and happy about our visit, and the Christmas spirit softened the hard surroundings. We never went anywhere without big bags of candy, but regardless of how many we took, we never had enough and felt grateful if we had just *one* candy for each child.

"How come Korea has *that* many orphans?" I asked after we had visited orphanages for several days.

"In Korea a child becomes an orphan when *one* parent dies, especially if it is the father who is gone. The mother has no way of earning a living and looking after her children at the same time. The Oriental culture makes no provision for widows or orphans. If a relative is humane enough to take them in, they become the unpaid slaves of their benefactors. South Korea lost so many men in the war that the streets literally swarmed with abandoned children. They would have died if the Americans had not gathered them up and fed them!"

Harriet explained it quietly and in such a way that the Koreans who were with us couldn't hear. I understood as the days went by why Harriet was so tactful. Koreans are very proud people and resent it that Korea has a worldwide image of miserable hopelessness and futility. They are grateful for all the help they've received but very eager to make it on their own in the foreseeable future.

"We hope to send money and help to other countries by 1980," the Korean national leader of the American organization, who hosted us, said to me with great dignity. "America has been very good to us and we shall never forget it, but we hope to become self-sufficient very soon!"

Although nobody would deny that America has put her imprint on Korea in many ways, it is very obvious that their Oriental culture will never become as Americanized as, for instance, that of West Germany did after World War II. Korea points proudly to a recorded history of 4,000 years allied to China, both culturally and politically, while maintaining its own independent individuality over the past centuries.

I could see more and more insurmountable differences as time went on. Very often it left me troubled and questioning, mainly when it came to those thousands of orphans and widows.

"Harriet," I said and wiped my tears after we had visited a home and school for the blind orphans, "how long do these children stay in those orphanages?"

"Until they are eighteen," she said.

"What happens to them then?"

Her face looked troubled.

"That's one thing we Americans are deeply worried about. Even now, after all the Westernizing influence, the present Korean culture is still most prejudiced and unyielding to those who can claim no family and ancestors. We try to train our orphans in vocational courses. They learn to embroider, sew, fix motors, cut hair, and other trades but we are fully aware that we send them away to a life of poverty and social rejection!"

Harriet's words dug deep into a sensitive spot in my soul. Within me echoed some words that were said to me before I left the United States. "Why do you worry so much about the orphans and the hungry people of the world? It's *their* problem if they don't control population explosion and poor economic planning! . . . Let them die and we will have less of a worldwide food problem. Why keep people alive for a miserable existence of poverty and struggle?"

I had glared at that "ugly American" and wondered what to answer. I had no answer except that I knew somewhere deep down within me that he was wrong. Or was he?

"God," I would say as I observed and ached, "could You show me the answer? I need it for my own peace of mind and for many fellow Americans who are as confused as I am—please, show me!"

The answer came to me on Christmas Eve. It was bitter cold. In the afternoon we sat in an unheated high school auditorium to listen to a Christmas program presented by a world-famous Korean orphan choir. The place was crowded, nevertheless. I could see the breath of people around me rising frozen into the air whenever the lights came on for intermission. My feet felt like ice lumps, and I shivered as I watched the little orphans perform. It was a flawless performance, and I tried to figure out how they did it. They changed costumes several times. Part of the time the girls appeared in sleeveless dresses and white socks, the boys in shorts. They not only sang like angels and clear as silver bells, they looked so radiant they warmed my worried heart.

That evening we were guests at their music institute and saw the choir's living quarters. It was obvious that these kids had more comfort than the many other orphans we had seen. By virtue of their talent they lived in a place that was moderately warm, and a big cake was waiting to be eaten after we had evening worship.

We sat alongside the wall, and I watched the orphans file into the dark chapel. The small ones came first and then the bigger ones, each one carrying a lighted candle. The Scripture readings were long, and several people gave speeches. We couldn't understand a word as it was all in Korean. I traced the dark silhouettes against the flickering candles while I felt strangely sad and forlorn.

I knew that I was homesick. I had never before been away from my family at Christmas, and I tried hard not to think about it.

I had the comfort of knowing that because we had come at Christmas to Korea a few hundred children would have a special treat for Christmas. We had left extra money for ice cream at the Lighthouse school for the blind and enough money for little individual gifts at places for handicapped and retarded orphans.

I was horrified when I found out that this year, owing to the decreased value of the dollar, several institutions had absolutely no money left to buy even the smallest gift for each child. The children received not even candies. How I ached for them!

I knew how it felt. My childhood knew of no Christmas or birthday celebration. I had listened to other children brag about what they had received, but there was never anything for me.

It made me feel good when I thought of the yarn and needles and the other practical little gifts that would be unwrapped by many little hands this Christmas because my fellow Americans cared. I had received several checks before I left the United States with the specific instructions to do something with it for some orphans. I was only too glad to do as I was told. It was only hard that we couldn't do as much as we all longed to do.

Here I sat musing and watching all those solemn young faces. The silence was impressive. The children stood or sat without as much as a wiggle for what seemed an endless time. Then came a humming tone, and the chapel filled with glorious sounds and melody.

Korean orphans sing like angels. Wherever we went, we listened to beautiful singing and music. Even the blind and retarded sang for us most movingly, but I had never heard children blend voices more perfectly than in that famous choir. They sang some songs in English, but most of their songs were in their mother tongue.

I tried to catch some of the meaning but Korean is so different from any language I know, I couldn't understand even a single word but one —Jesus. The Koreans pronounce *Jesus* as the Germans do: *Yay-zoos.*

That night the sound of that word floated again toward me as it had the days before whenever we listened to orphans sing. *Yay-zoos, Yay-zoos*

Suddenly I had my answer! "And it shall come to pass that whosoever shall call on the name of the Lord shall be saved" (Acts 2:21). The words of that text formed as clear as pearls in my mind, and I knew that God had spoken to me.

"Forgive me, Jesus," I said in my heart, "I forgot to look at it in the light of Your kingdom! Those orphans might never have a good life on this globe, but they'll have a wonderful time in eternity because someone cared enough to share rice and the Bread of Life with them. You died for them as much as You did for me, that we all might live, *forever!*"

That knowledge filled me with so much joy and gladness that it pushed all my homesickness and depression away.

I stood up and turned to the orphans: "Let's do something special tonight. Let's all sing together 'Silent Night, Holy Night.' You'll sing it in Korean, our American guests will sing it in English, and I will sing it in German!"

We did just that. I sang my usual high tenor part and Cathy, the black singer who had joined us that day, sang another tenor part. Tears ran down Bill's face as he came up to join us with his perfect whistling.

I knew that the angels above sang with all of us. I saw flickering candles reflect in shiny dark eyes, and the wonder of Christmas tied us all together in love. The evening ended with much laughter, hugs, pieces of cake, and American soft drinks. Before we left the party, those precious orphans had wiggled themselves deeply into everyone's heart.

I shall never forget them—nor the many other new things I learned from day-to-day while in Korea.

I didn't know how long ago the American influence began in Korean history until I was awakened early the next morning by the sound of church bells tolling. I looked at my watch. Four-thirty in the morning! Who was ringing bells at such an unearthly hour?

I began to ask questions a few hours later at breakfast and was deeply moved by what I was told. The bells ring every morning at the same time to call Korean Christians to prayer meeting. Before their meager breakfast, the people get up and go to the service.

I shivered when I thought of it. In the predawn of those freezing mornings those faithful people make their way to unheated churches to kneel on ice-cold floors to pray.

"How many Christians are there in Korea?" I asked Marlin, an American missionary who gives aggressive leadership and everything he has to spreading the Gospel in Korea.

"More than three million communicant members to my knowledge," he beamed. "South Korea is known as the most Christian nation of the world at this time!"

He went on to give me some of the background of the development of Christianity in Korea. Christianity was introduced into Korea by documents acquired in China by Korean diplomats in the seventeenth century. The first Korean Christians accepted the Gospel through the study of Christian literature.

Later, a systematic policy of isolation resulted in merciless persecution of Christians, who were considered dangerous by the government.

The closed doors of this "hermit kingdom" finally opened in the late 1800s, and American missionaries rushed in. They were not gladly received and suffered much from hardship and disease. Some Americans were martyred, like a missionary named Samuel, who was stoned in 1893 in the streets of Pyungyang.

From its geographical location one might expect that Korea's primary religion would be Buddhism or Confucianism coming from China or Shintoism from Japan, especially since at one period Korea was annexed and occupied by Japan.

However by their persecution the Japanese even helped to spread Christianity against their will in Korea.

Persecution is so very often a cause for church growth. Among the many reasons for the spectacular, rapid growth of churches in Korea is the unbelievable suffering the Koreans endured for so long.

During the Japanese annexation the Koreans were forced to observe Japanese Shinto rites and use the Japanese language. Many leaders of the independence movement against Japanese rule were Christians, which resulted in increased persecution of Christians.

When the Japanese left Korea after World War II, the Korean Christians thought that their days of persecution were over. It was not to be.

Five years later communistic North Korea invaded South Korea. At that time the church was much stronger in North Korea than in the South. Thousands of refugees, mostly Christian, from North Korea fled from the Communists to the South. Because of it the church was scattered in a way similar to the Biblical Pentecost, and in spite of great poverty and suffering new churches began to grow everywhere in South Korea. It is said that during the 1950s the number of their churches doubled.

I looked at Korea with new understanding after hearing Marlin's brief description of its Christian history. I could see the wounds and scars of war everywhere, but Christianity in South Korea is still very vital and alive, perhaps because of it. My heart went out to the Korean people. I didn't know for whom I ached more. Was it for the South Koreans who longed so deeply to share their new hope and faith in the God of love with those who were taught systematically to hate, or did I feel more sorry for their Northern relatives still living under Communism? Those in the North had but a slim chance ever to hear the truth; their spiritual eyes couldn't see anymore and their ears not hear and their understanding was strangled by the Communists' false teachings.

What did the eternal Great Shepherd say as He walked on this earth while His inner eye looked throughout the ages to the end of time?

"And fear not them which kill the body, but are not able to kill the soul: but rather fear him which is able to destroy both soul and body in hell" (Matthew 10:28).

4

The Merry, Mad Monks

I sometimes wished that Americans would fear a bit more than they do those who can kill both body and soul.

Americans often have a unique way of putting humor into the most humorless situations of their environment. That's a good way to make things go better, but sometimes it also masks dangers that need to be taken seriously.

I have a hard time smiling about anything that has something to do with Communism, but I couldn't help laughing when we stepped off the bus at the DMZ (Demilitarized Zone). The first thing I saw was a sign,

THE MONASTERY

HOME OF THE MERRY
MAD MONKS
OF THE
D M Z

"Bless their hearts," I thought, "it's more than a monastery that our GIs have to exist in out here—it's a bleak, ice-cold hostile Siberia, and ever so lonely and dangerous, too!"

Nobody talks about the danger, but it's there, and I could sense it from the moment we were loaded on the bus to visit the Joint Security Area near Panmunjom. It was tight security from the first moment on, and we were told not to take our special visitors tags off at any time. We were also admonished to stay with the group, not to smile or wave at the Communist guards, and not to get involved in any squabbles with the North Koreans. We also signed a paper saying that we were visiting the area at our own risk. The UNC (United Nations Control) could not be made responsible for the injury, mishaps, or death of any tourist. Cameras were allowed, but picture taking was restricted to several security areas; disobedience could result in smashed cameras and destroyed films.

Poor Ann put her camera away obediently whenever it was announced that picture taking was not allowed, which was of course always at the most interesting points of the area.

The DMZ winds itself 151 miles across the Korean peninsula from the Han River Estuary in the west to a point just below the thirty-ninth parallel on the east coast. It is a 4,000-meter (2 1/2-mile) wide stripe and largely undeveloped in the years since the truce was signed. In the center runs the Military Demarcation line. That line cuts off railroad tracks, streets, communication, and family ties. The area is supposed to be a buffer zone without military equipment and forces. Each side is allowed 1,000 personnel for administration of the Joint Security Area that we visited. The JSA is 800 meters (875 yards) wide and bisected by the Demarcation line, too. The buildings are set squarely on the line which runs not only through the middle of buildings but also divides the green felt-covered conference table within the conference building, where the Military Armistice Commission meets. Not more than 35 military police are permitted on each side at any given time.

As we entered a building, we were told that we could step across the middle of the room if we wished. You may walk on North Korean territory, but *please,"* said the American MP who was our guide, *"please,* don't touch the Communist flag."

I stepped across for a moment and felt sick inside—more so than I did all through that whole visit. I will always have a hard time looking at any Communist guard and relaxing at all!

The Red guards watched us carefully through every window, and tension was in the air.

"Please, don't touch their stuff, don't touch their flag," the American guide said again and again.

"Why not?" I asked our friendly MP soldier. "What's so special about it?"

The young man didn't smile when he answered: "The Communists have a thing about their flag. Whenever any Westerner or a South Korean touches it, they get so upset they either call a meeting to protest or cause squabbles and violations of the truce. So we try hard not to provoke them!"

"Those flags have caused us enough trouble," another young man of the American Military Police said with a smile.

"There was a time when each side brought in its flag through opposite doors to their joint meetings. Each day the North Koreans brought in a bigger flag—so the UN Commission would produce a bit bigger flag, too. At the end both sides arrived with flags so big and tall they couldn't get through the doors with them anymore. Finally they sat down to talk it over and come to an agreement. They agreed on a nineteen-inch flag. The Communists failed to mention that they would put three brass tiers below that flag. Since the UN had only two tiers the Reds ended up with the taller flag. The UN put a metal tip on top of their flag to match the other side, but the UN flag ended up a half-inch shorter than the Red flag. The Communists are very pleased with themselves!"

Most of the American tourists laughed as they listened and shook their heads.

"What childish games!" one woman said while she clicked her camera to take a picture of those controversial flags. I didn't smile, neither did I dismiss what I had heard as child's play.

It was a game all right but much more deadly than Americans can comprehend. I found out that fifty-three nations had responded when the game that was called the Korean War began in 1950. Sixteen countries furnished combat forces, with the United States carrying the major share. The three years of war exacted a staggering toll of many gallant men. When the truce was finally signed—after 225 "game" meetings had spread over two years and many more men had died—the world thought that the game playing was finally over; however, the Communists had only moved to a different stage of their game.

Yes, an armistice agreement was finally signed. Without speaking, Communist and UNC representatives signed, rose, and strode out opposite doors. But how long will it take the Americans to know that a signature and treaty mean nothing to a Communist? His desired end justifies *any* means in his eyes.

I listened and observed as I went from place to place and watched through Ann's telephoto camera lens. What I heard and saw was frightening to my personal experience and thinking. I was told that by 1972 the Communists had violated the signed agreement nearly 14,000 times but admitted to only two minor violations. As the Military Armistice Commission of both sides meet, the North Koreans make it a forum of their political propaganda and deny violations in the presence of proof and tape recordings. By now they have constructed a completely new railroad between Manchuria and North Korea and use it to ship in combat material. They build up their war power by land and air and deny it in the face of overwhelming evidence at the conference table.

Whatever the UN or the South Koreans erected in the security zone, the Reds built too, but a bit bigger! When the South Koreans, with the support of the UNC, put up a house and a special structure as historical symbols of their freedom and future hope of peaceful reunification, the North Koreans put up a similar building. It faces that South Korean freedom tower, but is much wider and very overpowering in structure.

I climbed the South Korean freedom monument all decorated with Christmas ornaments, and heard little bells jingle in the harsh winter wind while I looked over where the Reds patrolled and lived. There was not *one* sign of Christmas. They don't celebrate the birth of Jesus Christ, they don't believe in love and peace. They have *one* goal only: to make the world Communistic. I ached for them. People can be so dead sincere in their convictions—and so dead wrong. How well I knew! In the distance I saw what the North Koreans call Potem Kin Village (a copy of the South Koreans' Freedom Village). The oversized Red flag fluttered over it on a flagpole that seemed a mile high and could be seen at a great distance. New, white buildings form an impressive village. It is slightly larger than the South Korean village that is supposed to typify the comforts of freedom and free enterprise to the Communist world. I tried to get a good look at it through Ann's camera lens.

"That village is a ghost town," one American MP said to me, "we have watched the place for hours through our binoculars. There are no kids or animals to be seen, ever! Buses bring people in every morning during planting and harvest time and they work the fields, but they are shipped out every evening. Guards stay with the workers all through the day!"

I nodded grimly. I knew from past experience something about such *free* working conditions.

By contrast the South Koreans don't need guards in their village. Their farmers are very prosperous because the South Korean government does not demand army service of anyone who lives in the DMZ. Neither do they pay taxes. They are allowed to farm as much land as they feel capable of handling. They are the envy of many South Korean farmers who struggle with poor soil and high taxes. Nobody stops them from defecting to the North—they are welcome to go—but they stay.

Sometimes, we were told, the North Koreans will bring in busloads of young people and place them at the steps of their pompous white propaganda building where they chant and shout Communist slogans for hours. I saw pictures of it.

Many guards stand in front of such groups—strangely enough, none of the guards face with the group toward the UN buildings. The guards *all* face their own people, watching them closely. WHY? To keep anyone from breaking away and joining the other side, obviously.

Most American tourists who were there besides our group treated the whole deal as a funny novelty. They laughed a lot and clicked cameras without an end. They felt a bit annoyed when the Red guards brought visitors from the North into the Security building before our tour was through, and the MPs hurried us out with apologies.

"They've tried to harass us the last few days," our guide said. "They know it's Christmas for us, and they try to give us a rough time. We try to ignore it."

Most tourists thought that funny, too, but I didn't.

"What would happen if we had not evacuated the building when the Reds brought their tourists in?" I asked.

"We try hard not to have both sides in at the same time," the guide answered. "The Communists can become very obnoxious, and it doesn't set too well with American tourists. We have had to break up fistfights and hot arguments in the past. Americans are usually rather easygoing but if they get egged on too much, they *can* fight and they do! We try to avoid confrontation!"

That's typical of the American way of thinking, I thought. Unfortunately, the Communists don't think the same way at all!

Americans believe that it is wise to avoid provocation, to be tolerant and give in a little in order to hold the peace. That I can appreciate and admire as noble because I understand their way of thinking by now— but the Communists don't understand it as such. Tolerance, nobility, "giving in," they interpret as signs of weakness.

While we Americans boarded our bus to leave the DMZ (and most of my fellow-travelers had most likely already forgotten the little clashes and hostilities that had occurred), I had a pretty good idea what was happening on the other side. A big bus filled up with Communist young people. I knew for sure that there would be a feeling of triumph, propaganda speeches, and fists shaken after us. The North Koreans would return home exhilarated. They could report another little victory over those hated capitalists, those "weak" Americans.

I didn't talk too much while the bus took us back to Seoul. I tried to sort out my mixed emotions and feelings, and it was hard. I couldn't help but feel sorry for those brainwashed people. No Christmas hope, no love and joy, but hate and competitive satisfactions only. What a wasted way to live!

On the other hand, I couldn't help but feel defensive when I thought of it as an American. More than that, I felt frightened when I put myself into the shoes of the people in South Korea. What will happen after the North Koreans feel that their war machine is built up strong enough to attack again?

Jim, our tour leader, sat beside me on the bus. He turned to me and said over the loud clatter of the old vehicle, "Maria, did you notice that all our American boys at the DMZ are very tall?"

I thought back and nodded. Jim was right, I recalled; I had to look up to each one of them as I talked and asked questions.

Jim smiled and he had a bit of a friendly triumph in his eyes: "You see," he said, and sat up rather straight, "the North Koreans have that great obsession about having everything bigger and taller at the DMZ for propaganda purposes. There is one thing they can't control or add to—their body height. Koreans are usually taller than other Orientals, but they are still much shorter than Westerners."

I nodded. The size of the Korean people had often been the topic of conversation among us Americans in the last few days. It had to be taken into consideration everywhere, when shopping, squeezing into a car seat, or stepping through doors. Even Ann, our tiny Ann, had suddenly a new outlook on life; she towered over the masses of Korean people on the street.

"Well," Jim added, "all our Americans stand at least six feet tall or taller and it pains the North Koreans no end that they have to look up to our boys. At the conference table they make sure that their chair legs are raised enough so that they cannot be looked down upon!"

I laughed and shook my head. I knew it was no laughing matter, but I couldn't help feeling amused. Leave it up to the Americans to find a way to get even with the cantankerous North Koreans, I thought.

The United States soldiers I had talked to seemed to have more than a tall body but a tall inside, too. From the United States Major General down to the lowest ranks, those men have to live with belligerence, brazen lies, and provocation from day to day. Patiently, they try to reason, to avoid fights and arguments, to outlaugh hate and political game playing while standing watch for a free world. Merry, mad monks? No, they looked just like common all-American boys to me—but tall, oh, so very tall!

5

Because Someone Prayed

I couldn't believe my eyes. The big stone church seemed full to the last seat, and more people poured in through every entrance. We found a place in the section with the earphones where the Korean service would be translated into English.

Wherever I turned, I looked into a sea of somber, quiet faces. I had been told that we Westerners all look alike to the Orientals. It works the other way, too. I have a hard time seeing facial differences in an Oriental crowd; they all seem to have the same features, the same dark eyes and a similar hairdo. Everyone has straight, coal-black hair, even the older people.

We Americans stood out like sore thumbs with our gray heads of age and glory. The difference between us and them was not a genetical or racial difference, I was told, but a little bottle of black hair color. It could be found in *any* Korean home, even among the poorest refugees who lived in a row of tiny shacks we had visited the day before. It simply isn't done to appear gray in Korea until one is *very* old and desirous of being revered and respected as such.

In days past such an old, wise, gray-haired man would also wear a white blouse and white balloon trousers to signify that the days of manual work had passed for him. He also wore a high stovepipe hat made from horsetail hair, and his hair and beard were braided. Only a certain spot was shaved.

But such customs are no longer popular. Most Korean men now are dressed in dark Western suits. Some women wear long Korean dresses under their sweaters or simple winter coats. All of them seemed to prefer dark colors for church attendance.

"Why do the Koreans wait till afternoon to have their Christmas service?" I whispered as softly as possible to our Korean escort. The silence in that overcrowded place felt heavy, and I tried not to disturb the people around us.

"This is the *third* service since this morning; they will have another one tonight," the gentleman whispered back. "Every service is as crowded as this one. This church has a membership of more than 15,000 believers!"

The church also has several ministers, I found out, and they all took part in the service. Unfortunately, only some services were translated into English so we Americans had to sit and meditate since we couldn't understand Korean. We had plenty of time to do that. Koreans don't believe in any hurried religious activity, especially when it comes to praying or singing. My European background could identify with much of it. I had grown up with long prayers, black church outfits, and total silence during long worship services.

That afternoon in Korea Scriptures were read by passages and chapters, not by single texts. Hymns were sung with all verses, not the first, middle, and last. The opening prayer was given by one of the associate ministers.

I bowed my head and talked to God silently in my own language because I couldn't understand a word from the pulpit, but I ran out of prayer long before he did. So I decided to do some observing. Every head around me was bowed, most eyes closed. Nobody moved but the minister. He gave it all he had to give in word and gesture. I began to clock him. Minutes ticked by with no indication that he was coming to the Amen. I watched the people. No sign of unrest or impatience, just silent reverence and close attention. I wondered what we American worshipers would do if someone prayed longer than five minutes for opening prayer in our Western churches. The man in the pulpit kept on praying. Another minute went by.

Finally, I watched another minister get up, walk deliberately and slowly behind the praying, long-robed preacher, and tap him several times on the shoulder. Then he turned and sat down again. I held my breath. Would the man obey and finish? No, he didn't—my watch ticked another minute away, and he was still doing what seemed right to him.

My eyes watched the afternoon sun hit the upper window above the pulpit and light up the figure of Christ. I was glad to know that Jesus understood us humans. I wondered if even He was smiling at that moment, smiling at our funny humanness.

Well, the prayer did finally come to an end. I wondered if it was just my imagination and my personal attitude, but the loud Amen of the people sounded like a sigh of relief to me. The minister who had tapped his fellow preacher on the shoulder was the one who gave the Christmas sermon. He was obviously highest in rank, for nobody came to stop or tap him. He talked and read Scriptures and preached until the sun had passed the upper window. The church turned semidark in the early evening shadows. The people sat motionless and listened. Nobody slept, no child acted up. Several thousand people seemed to be in no hurry to have the service end, and I felt guilty about my own restlessness. It was very obvious that the Koreans love their churches. Yung Nak is especially reverenced, I found out after the service had come to an end and we walked down the wide stone steps to the street. It's a church of this century and was started by a handful of Christians who had to flee the North after the Communists began to persecute them.

When the Communists launched that surprise attack on Seoul early one Sunday morning in 1950, nobody expected it or was prepared for it. Seoul fell and the Reds wasted no time doing what they knew would hurt most those who had fled the North.

They packed dynamite into the church and got ready to blow it up. They got so far as lighting the fuse. The simple Korean church janitor, who felt it his duty to stay with the church after the others had fled, saw the spark work its way toward the explosives and he stopped it. He smothered the flame and the Communists found out. They took the little man in front of the church to shoot him. Before the bullet hit him, he fell on his knees to pray.

People nearby heard him and reported later that the dear saint had cried, "God, I am willing to die for You and my church. But will You reward my death by saving this church? Don't let them blow it up."

The bullets hit and his blood splattered the church walls and the stairs. The Communists made it a point to light the fuse again—and again—and again—and again. The fuse went out every time and the church stood unharmed when the Communists had to retreat back to the North.

I turned to look at the building as we left. What a memorial to God's willingness to answer prayer and to the power and prayer of *one* faithfully dedicated person who believed even in the moment of seeming defeat.

The church tower and the cross edged themselves into the cloudy, dark winter sky. I wasn't sure if these gray clouds of the north would bring more icy winds and bad weather before nightfall. But one thing I was sure of: Yung Nak, the church that stood because someone prayed, would be full again tonight.

The Korean Christians like to go to church, and they are eager to worship. They don't take such privilege for granted either—how could they? They remember and know only too well how fast they could lose it all again! There is just a prayer between them and persecution—no wonder they pray so much!

6
A Horn in the Dark

The battered Greyhound bus rattled along the southbound icy road toward Taegu. Korea may be beautiful in the spring or fall, but it surely has a spartan, austere look in the winter. The bare, brown hills or mountains are sprinkled sparsely with snow and every bit of water is frozen to its very depths. Little Korean villages and houses with their traditional, Oriental swing in the roof line nestle against or on top of many naked slopes; empty, dry rice paddies line the road, and a gray, murky winter sky hovers above.

By seeing more of the land I began to understand more about its people. Only a strong, tenacious people would survive—and the South Koreans have. The Japanese cut every tree they could find while they occupied Korea and carried the wood to Japan. Then the war tore even the bare earth into shreds and left the land desolate and wide open to erosion.

"Our organization has started a new project," Harriet said to me before we left for Taegu. "We are starting tree nurseries to encourage the people to plant some trees on their property. They have lived without trees for so long that they need to be reminded that trees and bushes protect the top soil from eroding."

I nodded. Well, we Americans should know after all the dust storms and loss of land we had in some parts of America in the past, when the woods were burned down or cut by careless settlers!

At least the Koreans' destruction was not by their choice! Nevertheless, preservation and the rebuilding of any land need much planning and care. Korea has a long way to go, but the people are willing to try and work hard at it.

I tried to imagine the rice fields green and the people working in them. That was difficult because there was hardly any sign of life anywhere except for the car and bus traffic on the road. As the late afternoon slipped into the twilight hour, the villages looked empty and dark. I knew why! The energy crisis was severe enough to discourage people from leaving the shelter of their sparsely heated homes to face the biting wind outside. Electricity was either too expensive (or nonexistent) to keep late night hours. People most likely huddled close together under a cover and tried to settle down for the night when daylight left.

I could have used a blanket myself in that old bus. The bitter cold numbness crept up my legs and I felt more and more chilled.

"Do you think this bus is heated?" I nudged Ann. She looked rather frozen, too. She didn't answer but looked with great interest toward the bus driver and the front of the bus.

"What are you looking for?" I asked, rather amused. "There is barely any light out there to see anything within or without—are you trying to take a picture in the dark?"

"You are right, there is *no* light out there," Ann said rather soberly, "I'll bet you anything this bus is driving without any headlights!"

"Oh, Ann," I grinned, "you are looking at the wrong side of life, just because you are sitting in the dark. How could any bus driver drive these treacherous icy roads without light? There is no star or moon out; it will soon be pitch dark, and he doesn't have cat eyes to see!"

Ann nodded grimly. "My dear," she said slowly, "remember the noise we heard just a while ago? We joked because it sounded like he had lost the motor! He didn't lose the motor but he lost whatever generates heat and light. If he has any light, it's his parking lights!"

I strained my eyes to see the headlights. Darkness was falling fast, and after a while I had to agree with Ann. That driver drove by the lights of the oncoming traffic! Whenever he passed vehicles moving on our side of the road, he warned them for at least a fourth of a mile that he was coming—and he passed constantly! That meant that his horn was in blaring action most of the time. Whatever light he didn't have, he made up for with ear-splitting noise. The horn seemed to be the only thing that was indestructible. It never gave out! What is there to do in a situation like that?

First I prayed. I knew that Ann did the same. I didn't know if the rest of our group had any idea what a hair-raising adventure we were in, but I didn't bother to find out. The bus was pitch dark, ice cold, and the screaming horn made talking next to impossible. So I prayed silently and thanked God that He would protect us.

Then I slipped out of my boots and pulled my feet up so that I would sit on them for a bit of warmth.

Next I stuck a finger into my good ear. (My right ear doesn't hear too well owing to a chronic ear infection during childhood, so I need to plug only one ear to shut noises out!) There are times when I count it a blessing that I am partially deaf! That night was one of those times!

With my ear plugged, my feet feeling cramped but warmer, and the deep assurance in my heart that God had promised us a safe return to America, I closed my eyes to meditate and reflect. I needed it. The days had been so full and rushed that I hadn't been able to digest it all mentally and to talk to God about it. I felt overwhelmed trying to remember all the impressions, tastes, smells, interviews, and happenings. There was too much going on too fast every moment of every day.

The winter winds howled around our decrepit bus, and the black darkness was less often broken by oncoming traffic lights as the night wore on. The bus seemed to have slowed down considerably.

"God," I said while I moved my aching body and my numb feet, "You have angels around this bus. Thank You for bringing us safely to Taegu!"

Everyone has his favorite Bible texts, and I have mine. One of them is Psalm 91. I repeated it quietly to myself while the bus slid over the ice and crawled through the dead of night.

"Thou shalt not be afraid for the terror by night; nor for the arrow that flieth by day" (Psalms 91:5).

7
They *Could* Live in America

Several night hours and a headache later I finally scrambled dazed out of the old, drafty bus and checked the headlights. Ann had been right. All the bus had were very dim parking lights. Nevertheless God and the driver had gotten us in one piece over icy, mountainous roads to Taegu —late but unharmed! Praise God, He had done it again.

Bill, the American missionary who waited for us at the bus station, shook his head.

"How could you come by Greyhound?" he scolded. "Didn't anyone warn you about their unreliability?"

"How can you say that?" I said and smiled weakly. "I was so sure that we would be in best care—after all, it looked so promising and all-American."

"There is nothing American about those buses here in Korea; I was told that the Koreans buy the Greyhound buses from the American bus company after they are discarded and declared unsafe for further use in the USA. You are lucky to be here; you could have sat at the side of a road all through the night!"

I shuddered in the cold night air and breathed a heartfelt thank-You to God for holding the bus together. We climbed into an oversized American station wagon.

I didn't know how much such a contraption could hold until I watched eight people and 19 pieces of luggage being piled on top of one another. I found out one thing: we warmed up fast! In spite of it I could think of only one thing while we drove to the hotel: my great need to find a hot shower, a decent meal, and a bed, but alas, we had arrived too late for the first two wishes!

The hotel bed did feel pretty good when I finally got to it, but I didn't get into it until the early morning hours. It wasn't until then that I understood that God had done more than one miracle that evening.

One of the main reasons why I had come to Taegu was to meet Dr. Howard. I had heard his name mentioned several times, and it was almost like Bob's name—the Koreans would say it with the kind of reverence they reserve for Bible characters and saints. He didn't look like a saint, not even like an American doctor, when I finally was introduced to him.

Doctors in America seem to carry an atmosphere of affluence around them; they usually smell, act, and look well tailored and rich. Doctor Howard didn't. He wore a very simple suit that wasn't very tailored. Maybe he had lost weight or he hadn't found the right size. It didn't really matter. From the beginning I was struck by his modesty, genuine warmth, and unpretentious, humble behavior.

He was only hours away from flying to the United States to attend his daughter's wedding. We could have missed him altogether if the bus had broken down, but he acted as though he had all the time in the world to answer my manifold questions.

He wasn't too willing to talk about himself, but his mission work— that was another story! His words came like water after the dam had broken, and his enthusiasm was invigorating. I forgot that I had no supper and that I was dead tired. That precious man poured his heart out, and his heart belonged to Korea.

Born of missionary parents and trained in the United States, he decided to go with his young wife back into mission service, starting in China and ending up in Korea during and after the Korean War.

Housing, medical supplies, and mission funds were meager, but the faith and devotion of the doctor and his wife were as deep and long as their daily working hours. They worked day and night to relieve suffering. As South Korea began to be rebuilt, so did the little mission hospital. One wing after another, one treatment room after the other. Story after story, square meter by square meter!

"We couldn't have done it without Bill," he pointed at his friend and fellow American, who had engineered all the building and maintenance, "and without the thousands of American people who send us their gifts year in and year out!"

I nodded. All those years I lived in the United States, I never stopped being amazed by the willingness of the American people to give. They give by their own free choice and will, without being forced or threatened! With my kind of background it may always remain a source of wonderment to me that a people by their own free will are *that* eager to share.

"The hospital is today a multimillion dollar complex," Dr. Howard said with a ring in his voice, "but that isn't our greatest joy. We have treatment centers and small clinics all over the Southern country, and out of that work we have watched 145 churches come about. The reason why we are not adding too many more churches lately is that Koreans don't believe in building churches too close together. *Any* Korean can walk at least four to six miles to a church, is their saying, so they will add on to their growing churches but not build new structures within the radius of six to eight miles of an existing church.

"It is exciting and so rewarding to be a missionary doctor," Dr. Howard said, "and God takes such good care of us. God provided me with an orphan flight to America so I can attend my daughter's wedding!"

"What do you mean by that?" I asked.

"Well," he said, "someone in the United States adopted one of our orphans and by law those orphans have to have someone in attendance going to the States. I am taking an orphan to the new American parents, and at the same time I will see my children and my dear wife. She has been in America for the last year. I can't wait to see them all!"

Some of what he said puzzled me. Yes, I could understand that he would be delighted about God's provision for his plane fare. He looked like someone who wouldn't have much of a savings account, because he put every extra penny into his mission work. But why was his wife in America and he in Korea?

A shadow fell over his friendly face. "We had sickness in our family, and she had to go to be with our daughter. I don't want to give you any details; I don't think my daughter would like it. Let me say just this much, sometimes it is hard for a missionary to determine where his first duty lies!"

"Isn't your first duty *always* to your mission field since God sent you?" I asked and meant it. To me, mission service is the highest calling anyone could get. Ever since I listened to the first mission stories at my foster mother's knees I have looked at missionaries as very special people sent of God by His own orders. Everything else had to be secondary and subject to that calling.

"Yes," the doctor said. "I have a similar conviction. Besides, I have wrapped my whole life around this hospital; it is my life work. Sometimes, however, missionaries are accused of neglecting their children. We have to send them so far away for their education. When a child gets sick, what is there to do? Do the parents drop everything and go to be with a child? I felt that I couldn't drop everything because this hospital has become too complex an operation and an important training center for native doctors and nurses, so we decided that my wife would be in America for a while and I'd stay on."

There was agony in that man's voice and face, and for the first time it dawned on me that missionaries have more conflicts to battle than I had been aware of so far. There isn't only culture shock, homesickness, and the suspicion of the natives to contend with. They must live with the many inconveniences and hardships of an underdeveloped land.

There are also loyalty conflicts, the guilts of neglecting either family obligations or mission duties. I wondered if on top of it such dear souls as the doctor and his wife were perhaps also wide open to criticism from various sources. I asked him about it.

"I'd rather not talk about that," he said quickly. He didn't need to; I had my answer and I ached inside.

Little did I know how often I would ache for the same reason in days to come, as I interviewed missionaries in various countries. I always took their side, of course!

I am glad I am not God. I wouldn't be as patient as He is. I would send a bolt of lightning at anyone who dares to gossip about or criticize our missionaries. They have their hands full without such unnecessary burdens as thoughtless criticism. I discovered so many more real burdens that are usually not even thought of as I listened, observed, and talked.

"God is so good," Dr. Howard said as he stood up to conclude our interview. "Everybody is well again in our family, and my wife will return with me to Korea after the holidays." His face beamed. It was obvious that he had missed her deeply and he couldn't wait to be together with her again.

"Tomorrow morning, or better, this morning," he looked at his watch and noticed that it was long past midnight, "I have to meet with the board for breakfast to hand them my resignation, then I shall leave for the airport."

"What do you mean? You are resigning?"

He shrugged his shoulders and looked suddenly very tired.

"You see, we missionaries find ourselves very often between the orders of our mission boards in America (and things very often look different to people in America than to us out here) and the native, national awakening of the land we live in.

"What I am trying to say is that the Koreans are very eager by now to lead themselves. The American mission board is equally eager to put all the leadership into Korean hands, but sometimes it is most difficult to make such a transition very fast."

"Do you mean that after you have wrapped your whole life around this hospital and built this place with American dollars, you now are signing it *all* over to a native administrator?" I asked.

"Oh, yes, and I am glad to do so," he said cheerfully. "My concern is that they will permit me to stay on as an assistant under the new native leadership. I want to help them in these many difficulties and unbelievable problems we so often face!"

I shook my head. What a spirit! We shook hands, and Bill took us back to the hotel.

"You'll never know how many problems the doctor faces from day to day," Bill said. "He is not a complainer. You see, we could never operate this place with the money allowed to us by the mission board in America. Especially since the energy crisis, our fuel expenses alone have gone sky high. You can't let sick people freeze! That man and his wife write hundreds of letters; they let their friends know what the Koreans need and it's by private donations from all over America that we are able to function! If the doctor ever leaves, the new native administration is in trouble." Bill looked troubled.

I spoke to the hospital staff through an interpreter the following morning. Most of them were Koreans; just a few people were Americans like the doctor and Bill. There seemed to be mutual respect and warmth among all of them, and I wondered if the doctor had set the tone by his own humble attitude and tactfulness.

I found out in many places that the doctor was loved. Miss Lee, who supervised the wing of the Children's Hospital, spoke with deep admiration about him.

"He is a great man and helps us wherever he can," she said with a big smile, "and we need so many extra things. So many orphans need surgery."

She showed us some of the stumps of legs and arms of children that had surgery scars.

"What happened to these poor things?" someone of our visiting party exclaimed.

"Oh, children very often get burned when they toddle too close to the open fire. Our Korean culture is not too eager to let cripples survive, but Korean parents know by now that they can leave unwanted or crippled children at our doorsteps. We find them when the doors open in the morning, hurt, screaming in pain, hungry, lonely, or just lying there, too afraid to make any noise, like little scared animals. . . ."

I wept, but not only because it was so sad and some kids looked so pitifully crippled and scared.

I cried when they all came on their crutches and by other means to the old piano to sing for us. "Jesus loves me, this I know. . . ." I cried and smiled and handed out candies and thought: "It is right to keep them alive. Someday they'll have perfect, new bodies and a mansion home in eternity because someone cared."

I thought it again and again as we visited homes for the lepers, the mentally retarded children, and for the handicapped.

"You know, we send many of our retarded youngsters to school," one nurse told me. "It's amazing how smart they seem to become after they have had a few months of regular meals and vitamins!"

I smiled. Yes, malnutrition can play havoc with the human mind.

"Tell me," I asked, "how come there are so few toys for all the kids around here?"

The American nurse spoke quietly, "Well, prejudices die hard—the native administration of our American organization has many demands to meet, and the dollars don't go too far anymore. Our retarded kids are always last on their list—so are the handicapped."

They were not last on *our* list, and they never will be! I made a mental note of it and so many other things in Korea. I knew we could not simply forget everything after we had left Korea. Yes, even if I had wanted to, I could never erase these many faces that have etched themselves forever into my memory.

I see them as clearly today as I saw them before me when our plane finally lifted shortly after Christmas to take us from Seoul to Taiwan. I was crying again, and I didn't apologize. I wasn't the only one, either. Ann had a hard time smiling, too, and so did the rest of the group. There stood Harriet among the group we left behind, waving, her slim face under the gray hair looking forlorn.

"I hate to see you go," she said, "it was such a special week for all of us here. Life out here often gets so lonely."

She wasn't complaining, for Harriet stays in Korea by her own free choice. She is there against the wish of her daughter, who wants her to be in America, enjoying the grandchildren.

Harriet lives in Korea because she believes that God wants her to be there. And so do Doctor Howard and his wife, and Bill, and Marlin, and hundreds of other Americans who *could* live in America if they wanted to.

I met so many people who *want* to live in America, but they can't because they were not born there. They dream and yearn for that land. But the American missionaries *could* be in America and make much money.

I tried to picture how rich Doctor Howard could be by now, if he had put all the talents and leadership qualities he has into moneymaking in the States. He could be so wealthy at his mature age—in dollars. But would he be as rich as he is now in inner satisfaction and the deep joy of knowing that a certain spot on the war-torn, suffering globe has become better because he gave his life to unselfish service? Someday he and thousands of others will hear the voice of God say to them: "Well done, thou good and faithful servant . . . enter thou into the joy of thy lord . . ." (Matthew 25:21). The same voice will also say: "Suffer little children . . . to come unto me: for of such is the kingdom of heaven" (Matthew 19:14)—and the orphans are coming!

8
Is Time Running Out?

"Hong Kong is rest time," Jim promised, and I was so glad! We all needed a few days of rest, at least I did. Itineraries that had not provided even a few hours for personal meditation and relaxation while visiting Korea and Formosa were rough on my hypoglycemia, and so was the starchy, spiced Oriental diet that had too many carbohydrates and so little protein to keep me going.

"No wonder so many Koreans have stomach cancer," I remember saying to Dr. Joon Lew, a Korean doctor whom I had interviewed shortly before we left Korea. He had smiled his polite Oriental smile and bowed as he answered.

"We do not know as yet why we have so much intestinal cancer among my people. We hope to find an answer for that someday, too—just as we are now very hopeful to stop Korea's greatest curse—leprosy!"

"You think you will *stop* leprosy?" I shuddered when I thought of the wasted faces with the missing noses, the arm stumps without fingers.

"Dr. Lew is world famous for his scientific research about leprosy," Jim had said. "He has found new medication to arrest that dreadful disease, and leprosy is not a death sentence anymore, at least not in Korea!"

Dr. Lew was the son of a Korean farmer, I found out, who had attended an American mission high school during his teens. At that time lepers were utterly rejected by Korean society and shunned, feared, and left to die.

"People thought that leprosy is highly contagious," he said.

"Is it not?" I always thought so, too.

"No, it takes years to catch it," he said, "and children of leper parents can grow up now without fear after we arrest the sickness in their parents by our medication."

"How did you become a leper doctor?"

"Don't call me that," he said. "My people are still too afraid to tolerate that word. I am a 'skin specialist' who operates a 'skin clinic'!"

"The skin clinic is under the sponsorship of our organization," Jim said quietly.

"And we shall be forever grateful for all the training, aid, and help we have received from America," Dr. Lew said warmly. "At a time when my own government was neither able nor willing to give me any help in my attempts to find a cure for leprosy, men like Dr. Bob and Jim," he pointed at our Daddy Jim, "have stood by and given me great encouragement and help. Now we have advanced so much that we are receiving worldwide recognition in our modern scientific studies. Now I am getting awards and honors from many sources, including my own government. But Jim was my friend when nobody knew me!"

Dr. Lew's words helped me to understand why Jim was so well known and loved in Korea. Jim had made visits to Korea numerous times since the Korean War. In his quiet, dedicated way he had come back from the Orient and gone to work for them. He had collected and sent thousands of dollars. He also shipped countless crates with food, clothing, and medicines given to him by his fellow Americans for war-torn Korea. Jim wasn't known only in Korea; he was known in Formosa and Hong Kong and every other country we visited. It was because he was so well known that it was so difficult for us to find some extra time for rest and needed privacy.

"Can't you attend just *one* dinner reception and visit the office headquarters for a few moments?" Jim asked.

Of course I did, and I ended up speaking and smiling and shaking hands and listening and being glad I did! How else would I have found out about Burma and that God was doing His work even in Burma today.

Roy, who had worked as a missionary in Burma, sat beside me at a Chinese dinner in Hong Kong.

"You eat too clean," he said to me. "You will hurt Oriental feelings if you don't spill something."

"What do you mean?" I asked, and looked at the spotless white linen tablecloth before me. Why should I deliberately spill something and make extra work for someone?

"The more you spill around your plate, the more you show how much you like the food," he said. "It's a Chinese custom observed in many cultures."

"How much there is to learn for Americans and other missionaries of other cultures," I said, "and how easily one can be misunderstood."

"Americans are *so* often so very much misunderstood because they are so very naive and self-assured. It never dawns on them that anybody could be offended by their behavior. After all, they *mean* so well." Roy rolled his eyes and smiled.

I laughed. How well I still remembered my own struggle with the American culture when I first came to the United States.

"At least you entered their land," Roy said. "The Americans had a right to ask that you adjust to *their* way of life. I wish they kept that in mind when they enter *other* cultures!" he sighed.

"We might never know all that happened to make Burma as hostile toward America as it is right now. When we were told that all Americans had to leave Burma, I was stunned. We had such a promising mission work going at the time; so many young people had responded to our invitation to attend our schools.

"Burma has pushed itself back into poverty and set progress back by many years. All the Americans who had to leave were trying to modernize the Burmese sugar and other industries. Burma had a complete economic breakdown when America was forced to pull out. But they are stubborn on the government level; they would rather suffer than admit their mistake."

"Has all the mission work come to a halt now?" I asked.

"No, thanks be to God, the adversity has in some instances more helped than hindered. The new believers seem to be so much more reliable and in earnest about their belief, and we are finding ways to return often enough to give encouragement and some aid. In the beginning we were not permitted to stay overnight at all, but now we sometimes find ways to stay for several days and nights. We also find ways to keep our training centers and schools going!"

My friendly fellow American laughed. "Every new obstacle becomes a new challenge—and we love challenges!"

"What about Hong Kong?" I asked, while the evening wore on and we had gone through seven courses of rice, fish, meat, and vegetables that had no resemblance to my favorite Chinese food I had learned to love in America.

"Hong Kong is another tremendous challenge," he said while I watched him spread some rice in a spilled fashion around his plate, "Chinese culture, English conservatism, a city of many trades, and a very uncertain future."

"What do you mean?" I *spilled* some of my rice, too, and grinned because I felt so foolish about it.

"Well, Hong Kong's English crown lease is running out in the not too distant future—what will become of this city then? Nobody dares to guess. We are so very close to mainland China, and Big Brother is too close for comfort. We might not have too much time left to evangelize—time may be running out!"

He wasn't the first one who had expressed such serious thoughts. I had heard those words in the days before while we hurried through Taipei to get to Hong Kong. In the blur of visits, talks, and appointments in Formosa two faces engraved themselves into my memory: one was Doris's and the other was Lillian's. Doris was blond and blue eyed and had come to the Orient at the age of seventeen. Her parents were German, but she was born in the United States.

"I read your book and identified much with it, Hansi," she said softly, "especially where you tell how you wanted to go back and see your mother before she died. You never made it. I didn't either, and it was my mother who encouraged me to stay. She believed so much in what I was doing, her heart was always with me on the mission field."

"What is it that you are doing?" I asked.

She was the founder of a Christian broadcasting company that worked through radio and television to reach not only the people of Formosa but those behind the bamboo curtain in Communist China. They have a fine staff of American and Chinese performers, studios, recording rooms, and a language school run by correspondence and radio.

"We are considered the best of its kind here in Taipei," Doris said and smiled. "The government workers learn English through us and even Chiang Kai-shek had words of appreciation for our work. He is a great person and believes in Christianity. We are so glad that things go so well lately."

"Didn't it go that well when you came?" I asked.

"No, it didn't go that well in the beginning. It all started with one little tape recorder, no money, a small slot of free time on a radio program, and much prayer, faith and enthusiasm.

"It is God's miracle power that got us where we are today," Doris said, "and we do not know what the future holds. We are so very close to mainland China."

"Is there anything we could do to help?" I asked.

"Yes, stay for a few months and help us," Doris said. "Write simple teaching material for our language school. We have such a hard time finding suitable little stories in English that appeal to the Chinese way of thinking. Or, leave us Ann; we need someone like her urgently."

I laughed. "I wish I *could* stay and help—but as for Ann, can't you send in a request to your mission board for a secretary? I am afraid I can't spare her!"

We all laughed, but then Doris got serious and a deep tiredness covered her face.

"Sure, we could get someone," she said, "but to find the *right* person is so very difficult. We have so many Americans, especially our young generation, who want to be missionaries, but most of them would do us more harm than good. I hope you'll understand that I am not critical when I say that most Americans are too sure of themselves. They are too convinced that *they* have all the answers, that *their* way is the *only* way, that they have an instant solution for every problem."

Doris continued, "You see, the Chinese are a very proud people. They look back at a history of several thousand years. They are deep thinkers, and they abhor rush and fast solutions. One has to adapt to their deliberate way of thinking *first* to find a way to their heart.

"It took me many years to learn to understand them, and I learned never to force anything but to wait. Most Americans don't know the art of waiting, and they try to force changes before it is time for them.

"We'd rather carry on as it is, with a staggering workload, than take a chance on destroying long years of patient work by one impatient, insensitive newcomer."

"Do you think Chinese or American?" I asked Doris before we left.

"Whenever I go home for furlough, I am accused of thinking and acting Chinese," she smiled a patient little smile, and her whole personality seemed to be surrounded by a deep serenity and ancient wisdom. "I do not know if I ever could fit again into the hurry of modern America."

Well, Lillian had one thing in common with Doris—an undefeatable spirit—but the rest of her looked different. She was very short and stocky; her skin looked like tanned, wrinkled leather, and her curly hair was a mixture of gray, dark, and light. Her eyes penetrated. She looked like someone who had climbed many mountains in the tropical sun. And that's what she had done most of her life, even now in spite of advanced age and a certain broadness.

She had come to Hong Kong in 1927 as a young bride with her husband to the mission field.

"We have only one life to live. Let's go where there is greater need." That's what she had said to her fiancé, and they came to Formosa. She was expected to keep her mission home up, to entertain, and to smile prettily while her husband taught, preached, and founded a theological college.

Lillian needed more than that for her pioneer spirit, a heritage of her Minnesota ancestors. She needed her own challenges.

The incredible poverty of the land, headhunting, floods, wartime bombing, the forsaken orphans begging on street corners, the lepers wasting away, the ignorance about cleanliness, TB, and the hundredfold sufferings screamed at her—and she decided to do something about it herself.

She rolled her sleeves up. She trekked into mountains where no white man had ever been before (let alone a lone white woman!). She helped, loved, taught, and even scared witch doctors out of their wits by her resolute, forthright bearing, and God blessed her efforts immensely.

Her husband finally died, but Lillian stayed on. With very simple methods of administration and very few paid workers she carries on a gigantic work of love.

"All you need is the faith of a mustard seed," she said, and her eyes burned into my soul, "and God will do the rest. Yes, nothing shall be impossible," she repeated to me and obviously believed it. "God *will* do the rest! We had many tight moments in the past, and we still do as the work grows.

"There were often times when we wondered where we would put them all and how we could feed them all. We care for orphans, the pregnant, unwed mothers, the mountain people with their blackfoot disease—but God and the American people have never let us down. A check will sometimes arrive at the last moment, but our prayers have always been answered."

"Are you planning to stay in this land?" I asked.

"If I should ever *have* to quit, my daughter and her husband will carry on with the work." Lillian pointed to a young couple and their small children, who were also with us that evening.

Her daughter had heard the remark and looked up.

"Mother, you know you'll *never* quit. You will outlive all of us!"

It seemed possible as I looked at that little five-foot woman who obviously defied age, space, time, and the devil with her mustard seed faith, her accordion to make music, and that soft, big heart under a rather crusty shell.

"You can't take on the whole world," someone had cautioned her once.

"I can't," she agreed, "but God can." They call her "Typhoon Lil" and I could see why!

"She has used the same kind of dress pattern for the last twenty years," someone told me, as we watched her stomp out with her determined walk and straight bearing. "She feels it's cheaper to stay with one simple pattern, and she sees no reason to waste a penny on changing fashions!"

I laughed. There was no danger with her about that. She wasted no money on hairdressers or paid attention to the latest fashions. That was very obvious. But there was an inner beauty about her, something that was out of the ordinary. It almost seemed that angels were at her shoulders—and why not? Yes, why not?

I sensed in her the same deep urgency I found among other foreign missionaries in every part of the Orient. It was an urgency that I didn't quite comprehend until months later when I began to understand why they all said it so often, "We don't know how much longer we will be here. We must do all we can!"

And so they work endless hours and give everything they have to that noble task of helping, healing, and loving while they wonder when and if the doors will close for them.

Doors had closed already in North Korea and in Communist China! Which country will be next? Will it be Roy's, or Lil's, or all of them? Is time running out?

9

Jet Fumes and Heartaches

The three days of rest we had expected in Hong Kong were cut short for us by the airline that would take us next to Saigon. Our flight reservations had suddenly been cancelled and to make it on time for another itinerary, we had to leave two days early.

"You mean they fly only three times the whole week and now they have even cancelled one of these three flights?" I was very disappointed and very American in my irritation. How did they *dare* to cancel our flight?

Well, they did, and nobody apologized for it either. I lost my chance to sleep late, to shop around, and to see more of the harbor and the city.

Instead we rushed to the airport hoping that we would get a seat. I was grumbling all the way. I had been fascinated by Chinese culture for a long time and had planned to see a lot of it in Hong Kong. I admire the Chinese way of life for many reasons.

No wonder the Chinese are a people of silent dignity. What a rich, ancient history they have! Their dignity seems to rest not so much on wealth and precious stones alone, although their dynasties had enough of them, but on wisdom, scholarly thinking, and that absolute defiance and triumph over time. Or was it perhaps a waste of human life?

It is hard to describe my feeling when I stood before needlework on which hundreds of peasants had supposedly worked a whole lifetime that they might make *one* tapestry to adorn *one* wall for their emperor. Thousands had tied knot after knot through endless years to make one beautiful carpet for the royal palace. It was more than my Western mind could comprehend! Inlaid work, almost too perfect to have been done by human hands, remained unblemished through the centuries, and we feasted our eyes on a mystic beauty that can be found only in the Orient. The China of the past had honored wisdom and logic in a special way, I was told. Every year great royal contests were given in ancient times where young scholars could compete with each other in the three great arts of Chinese nobility. They had to show perfection in poetry, the logic of chess, and music. The winner often was honored to such an extent that he would become the emperor's son-in-law or marry into other high ranks of the dynasty. Chinese men learned to desire wisdom as much as wealth! It is no wonder that China has written historic records since ancient time. It is also no wonder Chinese etiquette smiles and bows and remains silent while we Americans chatter and race through their galleries, take a few hurried pictures, and race to the next plane. They sit, and watch, and smile, and they are too polite to shake their heads while we run off!

The plane to Saigon had been stuffed full with people and luggage, the air felt stuffy, and the ride was bumpy. I was also hungry because the food I had eaten lately seemed to consist mostly of paper, glue, and other strange mixtures.

I wondered what Saigon's customs service would be like. The Koreans had been bears, looking for weapons. Hong Kong was a trade center and didn't care too much. Vietnam turned out to be the wave of a hand, but it wasn't our hand that did the waving. It was General Khang's, who had personally appeared at the airport with his wife to receive us. All he did was bark a command and snap a finger, and our luggage moved through like a charm.

Well, what gave us *that* honor? It was due to our fellow travelers, Bill and Virginia, and their kindness. They had opened their home in America to Mrs. Khang's brother, Hoc, who studied for a degree at an American University in the Midwest. They had opened their home to a stranger, and now we *all* received the benefits for it.

The general's limousine waited before the airport, and Bill and Virginia were ushered into it. No, they would *not* stay in the mission guest house with us; they were to be guests in the general's home! However, anything he could do for any one of the group, he would be delighted to do.

The Vietnamese people, I noticed, are by far shorter than the Korean,

Chinese, or Japanese people. The general was also short, but he surely didn't give that impression. He had a low booming voice and a very tall bearing. His wife in a beautiful native *áo-dài* (au-zei) looked like a tiny exotic flower beside him.

The general meant what he said, and our stay in Saigon was made much more pleasant because of his courtesies. After his limousine had rolled away, we piled into a van and were taken to the mission guest house.

We were assigned rooms and told to turn on the air vents if it got too hot. But what about the noise? The vent was bad enough, but the place was right next to a busy street, and Vietnamese vehicles topped their motor noises by just one thing: their smells! My room was facing the traffic and I knew I was in trouble—not only for sleep, but for my smog allergies and for my planned writing and note taking.

Ann marched to the housemother Joyce. "Can we find a quieter room for Hansi, please?"

"Yes, but that room would be hotter, less nice." Joyce looked apologetic.

I moved and we settled down. It was hard to imagine that my feet hadn't gotten warm for a week in Korea; the sweat poured from all of us. Saigon has a moist and sticky heat, and the air reeked from all the exhausts around us. Well, such is the joy of travel, whoever wants only comfort and ease must stay home (if that home is in America)! I didn't mind traveling as long as I could go home at the end.

"How long have you been here, Joyce?" I asked the missionary wife as we gathered for the meal.

"Oh, my husband and I came here as a young couple, and we have served in various capacities. Our children have spent most of their lives in the Orient."

"How can you stand the heat and bugs and . . . " someone started to say.

"That isn't the hard part of service in Vietnam," said Joyce's husband, a quiet, serious man. "The war is the great hardship."

Soldiers and guns were very much a part of Saigon, just as much as traffic-jammed streets, unbelievably smelly fumes, and thousands of Vietnamese on bicycles.

If Seoul was the city of taxis, Saigon was the city of countless bicycles. I tried to figure out how all those cyclists survived. Traffic rules in the Orient are simple: the largest vehicle always has the right of way and drives where there is room! Bicycles are no match for cars, but somehow they seemed to find a way, too. But how could the cyclists stand all those engine fumes? And *why* were most vehicles smoking like stovepipes, anyway?

Saigon had a motor oil shortage, I found out, and vehicle owners used just about anything to keep their engines oiled and running—even jet fuel! There had been a break-in at the airport, and many barrels of left-behind American fuel had been stolen. I had a hard time believing that jet fuel could smell that bad. I am convinced to this day that most cars in Saigon ran on castor oil and carried dead fish in their trunks!

Not too many people seemed to be worried about small problems like bad smells. They had much bigger concerns and perplexities to deal with.

I watched Joyce from day to day. She seemed so tired and drained. Sure, the guest house was full, and her children were home from boarding school, but her weariness appeared to be deeper than just physical exhaustion.

One afternoon I stayed behind while the group went to General Khang's house for tea. I had a sore throat and a bursting headache because we had been too much on the road that morning. Two hours of Saigon air was enough to knock me out.

Joyce came into my room and sat for a moment on my bed. "They tell me it was you who started the baby home," I said. (We had visited a very modern and efficient baby home of Jim's organization that morning.) "I was really impressed by the looks and efficiency of it."

Joyce smiled a tired little smile. "It wasn't always as modern as it is now. As a matter of fact, it started as a one-child project. Someone brought me a premature abandoned baby. She was so tiny and weak, I had to feed her every half hour and later every hour, day and night. I did it for ten days and nights, then I had to leave for a few days. When I came back, the baby had died. I promised myself that I would *never* go through so many sleepless nights and such agony again, but then," Joyce shrugged her shoulders, "what do you do when someone walks in with two babies who were abandoned? I had about twenty kids go through my home. Whenever they improved enough, I tried to place them either for adoption or in native Christian homes. In the spring of 1971 a small baby home was finally started. I went in July of that year for furlough to the United States and had a nervous breakdown."

"Did you work too hard?" I asked.

"Maybe I did," Joyce replied "but it was more the constant witnessing of insurmountable suffering that got to me, I think. I can't see the children suffer without going to pieces."

"What about your own children, Joyce—do they suffer under these primitive living conditions too?"

"My children like it in the mission field; they feel more at home here than in the United States. It's their mother who stews and worries and misses them," Joyce smiled.

"What do you mean by missing them? At what age do your children leave you to go to boarding school?" I asked.

"At six years of age," Joyce said quietly, "when they begin their first grade."

"You mean, they have to leave for elementary schooling?" I said aghast. "You mean, *all* your children have been in boarding school since their very first grade?"

"Yes," Joyce nodded, "and it's the same with each child I had. I try to prepare them from babyhood on for that separation. I worry if and how they will adjust, and at the end it's *me* who isn't adjusting. The children are doing great. It's a way of life for them. All our missionary children do it, so it's okay for them."

I shook my head. "I admire you people."

I remembered how worried I was when my daughter Hanna decided to go to boarding school for her high school years. She seemed so young when we put her on the plane at fourteen. I wondered what I would have done had I had to send any of my children away at age six!

"Don't say that," Joyce smiled sadly. "Not too many people back home admire us for it; we get severely criticized for it. So many church saints feel that we neglect our children and that we have no business being missionaries so long as we have growing children, at least not under such conditions. I feel so often torn and full of conflict. My husband and I have a deep conviction that this is the place where God wants us to be, otherwise I wouldn't have returned after I recovered from my breakdown. On the other hand we are condemned by our own church people in the states."

"Joyce," I said and fought tears as I watched tears roll down her tired face, "let me tell you something. I have watched it with amazement the last few years since I have been sent by God across America and the world. So many church people seem to *look* for something to condemn. If you were at home, they would find something else to hassle you with. It's unbelievable what some 'saints' can find fault with! It's tragic, but the conservative, evangelical churches are the only army I know of who shoot their wounded. Here you are, torn as a mother, trying to be brave and do your work for God, and they shoot you in the back for it. And to think that they do it in the name of Christ. They see themselves as right. They claim to be soldiers of the God of love!"

Joyce smiled again. "It makes me feel better when I hear you put it that way, and not all of them are that bad. When I returned to the States, I felt so desolate and depressed, I couldn't even sense God anymore. I had so many questions. I found no answers, but I found a friend. She didn't argue with me, she didn't condemn. She just *loved* me. God used her love and lots of simple gospel music to heal me. Here I am, three years later, back in the mission field, trusting God!"

She stood up because we heard a toddler cry. She opened the door and took a baby from a servant's arm.

"See this child?" Joyce said proudly. "We got her when she was two-and-a-half years old, or so we guessed. She couldn't walk or talk. She would just sit and beat her little head against the floor. Within weeks we had her walking and talking. She is now such a happy child most of the time. She is smart, too. Next week she'll leave for the United States to be adopted. I am glad that we will be gone when she is leaving. I'll miss her so much!"

I found out that evening why the missionary's family would be gone the following week. They planned to spend some vacation together in the cooler mountain region of Dalat before the children went back to Malaysia to their boarding school.

Since our itinerary listed a flight into Dalat but several days earlier, we asked if they were flying, too.

"No," the older boy said, "we drive up!"

"How come they let you drive when we were told we couldn't drive because the Viet Cong have made the roads unsafe with mines, road-blocks and sudden attacks?" I questioned.

"You'd better fly," the missionary said, "it's safer. But our children enjoy the drive, and we know a bit more what to do in case of an emergency."

"It's fun," another child piped up. "We are not afraid!"

"We watch the road carefully," Joyce said, "and when the traffic against us (from the north) stops flowing, we stop immediately and wait. As long as we see traffic coming, we know things are okay ahead of us."

I looked at them and wondered if Joyce was thinking what I thought. Most likely not; she seemed to be so happy in anticipation of a few days without the many responsibilities she carried as a housemother. Soon she would be only wife and mother at a place where it was cooler, cleaner, greener!

I still felt defensive for her. "I am glad those 'saints' at home don't know what's going on," I thought. "Maybe they would feel called to condemn again if they knew these parents were taking their children through war territories!"

Joyce must have known what I was thinking. She said quietly, "I do not think that we take any more risks for our children in driving up to Dalat than you do when you take your family into rush hour traffic in Los Angeles." She smiled and continued. "Aren't we all in God's hand? Isn't He able to keep us safe wherever we are?"

Suddenly everybody around the big table smiled and nodded. The little toddler on Joyce's lap smiled too. Why shouldn't she? She had a full tummy, someone loved and cuddled her today, and someone in America was waiting to give her a home and a welcome tomorrow. It felt so good to be alive!

10
Streetboys and Palace Protocol

Yes, we all looked forward to going to cooler, greener pastures like Dalat, but first we had to work ourselves through several more days of a very full itinerary in Saigon.

I was told that the average human mind cannot handle more than six hours of intense sightseeing and observation a day. After Saigon I wondered if I was below average. The mind isn't the only thing that can give out; a body can too, especially a stomach. My stomach has a hard time anyway, staying relaxed when things are hectic or something reminds me of past miseries. I am also not at my best when I am confronted by something like rats or lizards.

Rats were not the problem in the mission house in Saigon, lizards were! They crawled up and down walls and managed to come into the bedrooms, too.

"Don't mind them, they eat bugs," someone said. Maybe they did, but I had to forget their crawly looks in order to keep the butterflies out of *my* stomach.

Lizards were not the only thing that grabbed me in the middle. Human misery and suffering got to me until I felt physically and emotionally drained.

If there was one project that got to me more than baby homes, refugee work, and all the like, it was the homes of the "shoeshine" boys, homeless streetboys of Saigon who were gathered up and given a roof for the night. They also got a bed, some food, and perhaps the first human concern and care they had ever had.

In America we would call them juvenile delinquents, and to work with such boys is hard challenging work. I know because I had worked with high school dropouts in America for six years prior to my tour. In the Orient they are called streetboys, and the challenges are staggering.

It was another American war correspondent named Gene who began the streetboy work. After he finished his service with the American army, he returned to Saigon to work with an American organization for the betterment of those abandoned rag-clad youngsters, who tried to survive by hook or crook. By necessity it had to be mostly by crook or by ravaging through garbage. Sometimes they could earn coins by shining shoes, especially for Americans.

Gene was no longer in Saigon. He had gone to Japan for further training. But it just so happened that he had come back to visit at the same time we were at the mission house, and I caught his coattail before he had to leave again.

"Gene," I said, "how does one start such a rescue work?"

"It's simple," he said, "I befriended some boys as they shined my shoes, and I asked them if they wanted to sleep where I slept. I took five boys home with me, but those five told their friends and soon I had no more floor space left. We were offered an abandoned old warehouse by the government. My boys and I moved in and began to make a home out of it. We got some army cots and mattresses. We built a cooking place to boil big kettles of rice—but we could never stay ahead of the demand. One boy would tell others, and they came by the hundreds to us."

"What seemed to be your greatest problems in this type of work?"

"To teach such boys some kind of discipline and order. They also have a hard time grasping the Gospel story of love. They don't know what love is; they grow up worrying about one thing: how to stay alive for one day at a time!"

"They are suspicious, they fight, they try to outsmart, they lie, steal; they have to be taught the most basic principles of hygiene and human interaction."

"Is it worth the try?" I said and regretted the question while I asked. I knew better.

"I think so," Gene said. "We have seen some of the boys who seemed the most hopeless change so drastically that I can't believe it myself. We simply do our best and leave the rest up to God. We might never know until we are on the other side with God how much or little has been done. Who can say what can happen in the life of boys like these after the seed of the Gospel has been put into their young minds? They might remember years later and turn to God when all else has failed!"

I thanked Gene for his time and later I had a chance to talk to Paul, who was the present director of the streetboy work.

"The streetboy work is changing its approach by now," Paul said. He drove us proudly to the outskirts of Saigon and showed us what such boys could do if given a chance. From the boards of crates and boxes that had brought food, clothing, and medicine from America to war-torn Vietnam the boys had built a *home* for themselves. It stood on a plot of land that also gave them a chance to raise pigs, grow vegetables, keep chickens and other fowl, and best of all, it kept these boys busy and out of mischief and crime. It also gave them a sense of pride and belonging. After all, it was *their* home, they felt responsible for its upkeep and enlargement and they learned important skills in the process.

"We hope to have more garden space this summer, and the boys will be able to grow more of their own food. Most of them love to work with the soil. They have never been in the country before; all they knew was filthy city streets!"

The last thing Paul showed us was a home for refugee boys. "We have found that it is wise to keep the *good* boys who have just recently lost their home apart from those who have lived on the street most of their lives. A good kid can turn bad much easier and faster than a rotten kid may become good. If we keep those with a good behavior record in one home, we have much better success!"

"I wish you could convince American social workers, judges, juvenile delinquent courts, and others of that fact," I said. "It bothered me all those years I taught. In America we throw a youngster who just goofed or did some dumb thing together with all kinds of criminals, and those kids learn all the wicked things they didn't know before, while staying in juvenile halls or prisons to be 'corrected.' "

Paul nodded. "We learned it the hard way, to keep the hard-core streetboy and the innocent refugee fellow, who has only lost his home, apart. Since then we have a much better chance of reaching our objectives for our boys."

"How do you know the difference?" I asked.

"We try hard to record each case history and that gives us an idea," Paul said. Then he asked: "Would you like to see some of our case reports?"

I did and my heart ached. Some boys had watched their parents die, or being shot, or a mine had blown up, or a relative had tried to look after them—or they knew *nothing* about their family's whereabouts.

"They are ours until they turn sixteen," Paul said quietly, "then the government takes over. They need every soldier they can get."

"Oh, Paul, not so young," I said, "they are mere children!"

"To us they are, but South Vietnam is desperate! There is a law here that doesn't permit *any* boy to leave the country to be adopted out to another land; they want to keep every male in Vietnam."

Paul reached toward a skinny, short boy who looked to me like a twelve-year-old child. He said something in Vietnamese, and the boy stretched his hand toward me.

"This boy just came back from the fighting line. He is on sick leave because he was shot in his hand. He has no other place to go, so he comes back home to us."

I looked at a small boy's hand shot through by a bullet—the wound was almost healed, and I found myself wishing that it wouldn't heal so fast. As soon as the hand was healed, this child had to go back to war. I cried my ever-ready tears again, and the boy looked puzzled. I knew that he wondered why I cried. It would never have entered his simple mind that I cried over him. Why should a strange American lady cry for him or any of the boys? How should he know that mothers cry when they see kids hurt? He never had a mother, not even a mother image —most streetboy homes are run by men! It was something that bothered me deeply and I said so.

Paul shrugged his shoulders. "We are aware of the many shortcomings in our program, but we do the best we can under the circumstances!"

The evening after we returned from seeing several streetboy homes, I had been invited to speak at the International Church. I was utterly exhausted that night, fighting a bad cold, and my throat hurt so badly I couldn't swallow. It was obvious that the smog, or whatever it was, was getting to me. A Chinese choir performed, and by looking around it was clear that I was speaking to people of various races and nationalities.

"Give me Your words, Oh, Jesus," I pleaded, "I don't know what these different people need and how they will interpret my words!"

I spoke on something I had never spoken on before in the same way: how to overcome fear and hate. I knew something about such things. Hate had once been the driving force of my shattered life, and fear was something I still battled with from day to day. But I also knew how it felt to be securely in the hollow of God's hand and to trust Him when I couldn't see past the next moment or step.

After the service a missionary lady walked up to me. "God bless you, Hansi," she said warmly, "the Holy Spirit spoke through you. You cannot even know what I am saying since this is your first visit to the Orient—but nobody who has been in this land for a long time could have spoken with more directness, sensitivity, and tact. You see, *one* wrong word or statement could have erased the good of your entire message. Only the Holy Spirit could have told you what to say and say it in such a way that you didn't offend *any* one of the many nationalities assembled here—you said it just *right.*"

"I didn't," I said and choked up again, "it was God all the way!"

Paul walked up and said: "Your message helped me so much. There are so many concerns we carry; the dollar has lost too much value, and I often wonder how we will feed all our boys on the little budget we have left."

"Paul," I said, "remember, we Christians don't depend on budgets, we depend on the promises of God. Don't ever forget that we have a *rich* Father. He owns the cattle on a thousand hills. As Corrie ten Boom would say, 'He will just have to sell a few extra cows for your streetboy work.' "

I saw Paul the next day and he beamed, "God did it again." He smiled his boyish, shy smile. "God *did* it. We just received food supplies for another three months, our freezers are full."

"What happened?" I jumped with excitement.

"The food came from a completely unexpected source," Paul said. "The American government is pulling most of its civil service people out of South Vietnam. Most of them have already left. The government's red tape, however, is slower than the people who followed pull-out orders. It means that food supplies have come in for them after they were gone. Instead of taking it all back to the United States, the government divided it among American charity organizations, and we got enough to feed our boys for the next three months!"

"Praise the Lord," I said and gave the young man a big squeeze, "God knows also what will be needed after the next three months! He knows the future!"

I am glad that Her Excellency, the First Lady of South Vietnam, Madame Thieu, didn't know what was waiting for her in the future when I was granted an interview with her in the royal palace the following day.

I couldn't believe it when Don, a burly, tall Canadian who worked with Jim's organization in Saigon, announced the planned visit to me.

"You mean, I am going to visit the president's wife?" I asked.

Don's mustache broadened over a big grin.

"Yep, and you'd better get a few instructions about Oriental etiquette and palace protocol fast!"

"Okay," I said and tried to collect my thoughts. "What do I wear?"

"No question, Hansi, you have become totally Americanized," he laughed. "Any full-blooded American woman would ask that question first! Business attire is appropriate."

"What else do I need to know?" I asked.

"You address her as 'Your Excellency' or as 'Madame Thieu,'" Don added. "Your seat and every other seat will be shown to us by her interpreter. You will be the guest of honor and sit to her right. She will enter after we are seated and leave before we leave!"

"Gulp," I said. "We'll try to do our best!"

Several limousines took us to the palace. Don sat with the driver in the first car. I sat alone in the back seat. It wasn't "proper" to put anyone else with me. I tried to look serious and important. At the palace I followed a uniformed official to the inner chambers of the First Lady. The rest of the party followed at a respectful distance. I tried hard to behave and not to look back or fall over my feet. It seemed easy, the carpets were so thick and bulky.

"God," I prayed, "why would a little girl who grew up sleeping in a hayloft be asked to walk into a royal palace as a guest of honor? Who am I, Jesus, that You would arrange that for me?"

"I honor those who honor Me," God seemed to say, "you *are* the daughter of a king!"

"Lord," I prayed again, "may I honor You in everything I say; let me be a friend to that woman!"

The room where we Americans were seated was breath-taking in its beauty. The tapestry, the carpets, the carved furniture reflected a blend of French and Oriental richness that stood in strange contrast to the barbed wire, the dirt, and the poverty I had seen the last few days. The whole thing reminded me of a fairy tale—until the First Lady walked in.

I didn't know that the interview was going to be on national television news—but floodlights clicked and cameras purred, and there were smiles, handshakes, and introductions. Then the TV crew left, and we sat down to talk.

I liked Madame Thieu from the first moment. She was a beautiful, gracious lady whose deep dark eyes spoke of suffering and loneliness. We talked for seventy minutes. It was obvious that we liked each other and that we felt a bond of sisterhood. Why not? She and I believed in the same God. She was a devout Catholic, I a Protestant, but we both claimed the same Jesus Christ as our Lord. She told me about her humanitarian work, I told her about my writing and my travels. Her interpreter was fast and fluent. I spoke English; Madame Thieu replied in French.

"Madame Thieu, is there anything I can do for you and your country?" I asked and meant it.

"Yes," she said and her eyes darkened with pain. "When you return to the United States, will you please tell your president and your press that they shouldn't tell such exaggerated and distorted news about South Vietnam? We have enough problems already; why would the American news media be so cruel to us?" Her eyes pleaded. I swallowed hard.

"Madame Thieu, I am sorry," I said. "You see, the American news media is one of the prices we pay for our freedom!"

Her eyes had a puzzled look when the interpreter got through talking. I knew we hadn't communicated on this issue and I knew why. It had taken many years for me to understand the American way of life, especially the meaning of freedom in relation to the American news media. I finally learned to understand that for everything in life there was a price to pay—even for freedom as America had it.

Freedom can be misused, but if one tries to control misuse of freedom, it destroys freedom. The American news media thrives on that principle and gets away with almost anything. To preserve freedom Americans put up with it; but how could that be explained to a woman like Madame Thieu? Her background was so different! Her thinking had been formed by a culture that knew little about individual or national freedom. Her woman's role was based on centuries of Oriental philosophies that put her into a subservient role, regardless of social rank or title.

I didn't even try to explain it. I just changed the subject.

"Madame," I said, "is there anything else we can do for your people?"

"Send us wheelchairs," the interpreter translated, "please, send us many wheelchairs!"

I looked at Jim and Don. Don spoke up: "Your Excellency, we were not aware of that need; tell us more about it."

"Our need for wheelchairs has increased sharply since the American troops left. Since we are so short on fuel, our wounded cannot be brought in fast enough from the fighting front to save their limbs after gangrene sets in. Our doctors must amputate so much. The guerilla warfare does us much harm, too. The Viet Cong plant mines in the most unexpected places; it's usually legs that are lost by the people who step on mines. All these people are condemned to a life of complete inactivity unless we can give them some kind of mobility. We do not care how simple in design, just something that moves so they can make a living."

"Madame Thieu," I said quietly, "I will try everything in my power to get wheelchairs for your people!"

I meant it, although I had no idea where to begin. I knew I could find out. Somewhere fellow Americans would be willing to help out. They would back me up in spite of what the news media said. I could trust God and those many Americans who still would rather help than condemn or hurt. I was so sure of that!

"We'll send wheelchairs as soon as we can," I said when we finally had to say goodbye. It was with reluctance on both sides—she and I had become friends.

Whatever the American press had to say, I knew that I had met a beautiful person. Her heart was full of deep concern for her people, and she tried to do her *very* best under *very* tough circumstances.

She turned once more at the door before she walked out and waved at us. I do not know if it was in the protocol. All I know was that her dark eyes were full of sadness and pleaded for friendship. I wouldn't forget that pensive and lonely look—ever!

11
Gifts of Friendship and Love

Don smiled his contagious smile again. "Hansi," he said, "the visit in the palace is a record. Her Excellency isn't in the habit of giving seventy-minute interviews. She is usually very brief."

"I didn't know that," I answered, "it seemed to be so natural that we wanted to talk as long as we did. She and I are friends."

He nodded. "That was obvious! Look how eager she was that we might see her hospital, too!"

We did visit her hospital the same afternoon. It was a modern, high-rise building, and the native doctor who guided us spoke English fluently.

"Two wings are not opened yet because we do not have enough supplies and personnel," he said, "but we hope for the best. If it were left to Her Excellency, we would treat only the poor in this hospital, but we must keep our high expenses paid so we cannot afford to keep more than one wing for the poor open." Then he led us through "her" ward.

We found them everywhere, in every bed and corner, lying, sitting, hovering: the old men, the crippled peasants, the young mothers with newborn babies. They were all mixed together in one ward. They smiled at us with toothless grins and shy nods. Everyone seemed so glad to be inside while others waited in long rows to be admitted whenever a bed became free.

I couldn't get used to the loud and horrible wailing of the bereaved families wherever there was a death. The poor ward of the hospital seemed to ring with crying and screaming all the time we were there, and I wondered if it wasn't hard on all the other sick people. If it was, nobody said so. "It would be unthinkable *not* to wail and mourn," Don said. "The more people cried over a dead body, the better, and the more the dead were honored."

In America the doctor would have the whole family under sedation if they were to carry on like that, I thought. Maybe it's good for human beings if they are permitted to express mourning so audibly. I realized that it wasn't done for emotional release only but as part of their ancestor worship. The dead play a tremendous part in the daily life of the Vietnamese people. Most of them are Buddhists, and I watched even the beggars at street corners burn their little sacrifices and food offerings to appease the dead. It was a most important matter not to be the last in a family line. Who would look after the ancestors and himself if there was nobody left? Who would wail?

Just before we ended our visit in the hospital, I received a lovely gift from Madame Thieu. We had been ushered into her office. I expected it to be another round of drinking tea. Wherever we appeared in the Orient, we had to drink a cup of tea. If we visited ten different institutions in a day, we drank tea ten times a day. That afternoon Madame Thieu had sent gifts for every lady of the party. Everyone received a lovely lacquer box, and I was handed a huge picture. It was wrapped and very heavy. When I unwrapped it, I discovered it to be very beautiful. I thanked the interpreter who had been sent to bring us the gifts, and we marched back to our cars.

Don had such a keen sense of humor, but I never laughed more about his funny stories than that evening when General Khang gave a special dinner reception in our honor. By then even Ann's stomach had learned to tolerate some of the native foods, and I had learned to enjoy most of the many courses. One dish, however, I couldn't bring myself to eat. I couldn't believe my eyes when the waiters brought it in. It was a whole little piglet, roasted to a caramel gold brown, its mouth wide open to hold a whole apple. It even stole the show from a baked rooster with a battery-operated light inside its head, so he could watch with illuminated hollow eyes how his body was cut up for culinary delights.

I managed to eat a piece of the bird—but that little baby pig got to me.

"Taste the skin," Don said, "it's a native delicacy. They brush the skin with honey and roast it to candy brittleness; it's delicious!" I tasted one little bite. It had the consistency of a greasy but hard caramel candy. The skin was served as a separate course; after that the meat was cut up and offered around.

During the meal reporters tried to come in for pictures, but the general ordered them to leave. I wondered why. By the end of the meal I found the clue when I heard Mrs. Khang say to Don, "Thank you, thank you for all your good words. I haven't seen my husband so happy and relaxed in many months."

We avoided upsetting topics that evening and didn't discuss the political situation of Vietnam. The only time we talked about Communism was when Don asked the general if he had heard about the private discussion that had taken place in the Kremlin at the last visit of our American president. The general looked puzzled.

Don kept his face straight. "Well, Brezhnev asked our president how he had slept. The president answered that he was sleeping just great in Moscow. Then Brezhnev said, 'I had a dream, Mr. President. I saw a Red flag flying over your White House in Washington. On it, it said 'Long Live the Proletariat.'

"Our American president smiled. Then he said to the Russian leader, 'That is very strange—I had a similar dream. In it I saw the Red flag waving over the Kremlin.'

"Brezhnev said, 'What's so special about that? We have had the Red flag flying over the Kremlin ever since our revolution. What did it say on the flag?'

"Our president answered: 'That's what I couldn't figure out; you see, I don't know how to read Chinese!' "

The general laughed so hard, he had tears in his eyes.

We all laughed and made light of it, but deep inside we all knew that Communism was no laughing matter. Oriental people live with that threat and fear day in and day out. I, too, had a hard time forgetting how close we were at all times to guerilla warfare and Viet Cong attacks. That worry became actual danger the next day when we finally flew from Saigon into Dalat.

What the missionaries in our guest house had said about the place was more than true. Cool, green, and ever so beautiful a place, Dalat had been a famous resort area during the French occupation, and the Americans favored it, too.

A middle-aged American missionary named John picked us up at the small airport, and we packed ourselves into a large vehicle.

"We are taking you up to the Montagnards at the village of Sut Thong," Jim explained. "It's dangerous because the Viet Cong are walking the jungle that surrounds the village but I feel it's something we *must* see! 'Montagard' means God-follower, you know."

I did not know, but I nodded and watched the green dense foliage fly past as the car climbed up into the mountains. The coolness of Dalat gave way to more heat again, and when we arrived at the village I understood why. Sut Thong sits flat and shadeless on the top of a hill, surrounded by jungle mountains. The tropical sun broils the village and the fields that sustain life for the villagers. What many strange sights we saw!

The entire village was surrounded by a deep moat. In place of water it had pointed bamboo sticks on the inner side. The needle-sharp points had been dipped into strong poison, I was told. Behind the moat appeared a kind of hedge made from more sticks, barbed wire, and strings, and overgrown with jungle thicket. The only way into the village was by one large gateway. A young boy, his gun leaning against the open gate, stood guard.

He must have recognized John and his vehicle a long way off. His face beamed with a broad grin and the village people were assembling to welcome us, as we arrived inside.

I felt bewildered and sick again. The heat, the smells, and the stinging poverty in the village grabbed me right in my stomach, and I fought both nausea and tears.

We were surrounded by smiling faces, outstretched hands, and nearly naked kids wherever we looked. The Sut Thong village had a happy occasion, a feast, a time to rejoice. Their beloved friend and white father John had come, and he had brought with him friends from the land across the sea they all had heard so much about.

So I smiled back and shook hands and tried to look happy, too, but it was hard for me. I knew much about poverty myself from times past, but I had never seen such bare subsistence and destitute living before. There were small, primitive grass-thatched bamboo huts, dry, brown, dusty trails, a few pigs, cats, and chickens amidst the many dark-skinned people. Most of the people were very short, thin, hollow-eyed, and obviously well acquainted with hunger, but oh, so happy to see us.

"This is Sau, the leader of the village." John introduced to us a short, slender elderly man with black curly hair and a broad smile.

Here was another short man with very tall bearing and a quiet dignity. I could sense something special about Sau; he seemed to radiate strength, confidence, assurance—more than that, he carried an aura of peace about him. He had donned suit, shirt, and tie to welcome us. So had his younger brother Kar, another leader of the village. I wondered how they could stand to be so formally dressed in the heat. To them it was obviously important to wear the best they owned in order to show us proper respect. They perspired profusely.

Suit and tie were not the only demonstrations of their genuine pleasure to have us there; their wives also prepared a meal for us in the chiefs' house. Sau and Kar lived together in a house bigger than most of the huts. It had a crude long table and benches and some simple marks of civilization like a colored print on the wall. There were a few hooks to hang up pots and things and it had more room than the average huts.

We were ushered into Sau's house with great ceremony and asked to sit around the table. Kar and Sau would eat with us. But what about the others? They looked through every window opening and door and *watched* us eat!

Ann looked at me. "I feel terrible eating their best food when we know how hungry they often are," she said under her breath.

"I know," I nodded, "but Jim says that we would hurt their feelings terribly if we declined."

So we all sat down and ate. A chicken had been boiled for us. A vegetable soup smelled delicious. Salad greens and vegetables had come fresh from the field, and mountain rice, corn, and squash had been steamed just to the right, sticky consistency.

I decided to eat only the boiled stuff and not too much of it. Too many hungry children watched us too intensely. They seemed to taste every spoonful of all those delicacies with us; some even swallowed when we did! I didn't dare to touch the raw stuff, as much as I missed fresh salads by then. The danger of infestation by intestinal parasites is acute in the tropics, and I knew better than to take a chance.

I also knew that the "left-overs" of the meal would be served to the rest of the chiefs' families after we left. We tried hard to "leave" as much as possible! Who wouldn't have? Kar's family alone consisted of twelve people, Sau had two sons, and beside the children stood the old people—waiting!

12
A Fort of God

When John took us to Sut Thong shortly after Christmas of 1974, the people had lived there for more than seven years. War had torn through all of Vietnam for more than thirty years, and we could see old and fresh wounds everywhere.

"The Central Highlands have suffered drought," John said quietly during our meal there. "This village is the only one that harvested some corn and rice at all. Nevertheless, they adopted eighty-three war orphans on top of their own children and share the little food they have left with them.

"These people have a great spiritual way of life; they take the Bible literally. They appear defenseless, but they are a fort of God against Communism. Other villages have collaborated with the Viet Cong; this village has *never* helped the enemy—either willingly or unwillingly!

"All they have are some light guns and a few shells given to them by American soldiers before the GIs left; they have no protection against enemy mortar and rockets, but their shield is faith and prayer. They trust in God and keep their powder dry."

They also smile and play their gongs and give radiant testimonies, I found out.

"Every mountain village treasures its set of brass gongs," John said. "You can hear the deep resonant tone echo from the mountains on every important occasion."

Our visit set the gongs in motion. The pastors and village elders beat a welcome rhythm for us, and the valleys rang. I wondered how many Viet Cong heard the gongs, too. The villagers didn't seem to worry about it. They had stood their ground against fear and endless years of harassment, and in the bitter reality of war they had learned to live one day at a time. Up to the day we visited, the enemy had been defeated; why spoil the day by worrying about tomorrow?

The deep, big hole in the middle of the village reminded and reassured the tribespeople of God's protecting power. "The last attack by the enemy was hard," Sau said in his testimony. "They broke into the village, and we had many hours of battle with the Communists. Those of us who had a gun, fought; the rest gathered in the big hole for shelter. They helped us, too! They sang and prayed.

"After ten hours the enemy soldiers retreated. Their losses were heavy; they dragged their dead and wounded with them. The guerilla leader had been killed, and we found him stuck in the pointed sticks of the moat. We buried him outside the village. This is the canteen he carried on his side." Sau handed me a beat-up aluminum container that looked as though it had seen better days in the U.S. Army.

"When the fight was over," Sau continued, "we gathered our people together and counted heads. We had lost one mother and a child hit by a mortar, and three of our fighting men. Everyone else was unharmed. Our God had fought for us again as He has for all these many long years!"

"Yes, God is with them," John nodded after Sau had finished his testimony, "but those people have an incredible boldness and courage because of it. Look at that man," John pointed at one of the men who had played the gongs for us. "This is the famous one-time sorcerer La Yoan. Someone told me that he never wasted a shot. Every time he would aim, he would pop up and shout: *In The Name of the Lord God Jehovah*—and he never missed! He made his few shells last ten hours!"

La Yoan smiled at us.

"I arrived one hour after the Communists had retreated, and I found the village people in their four churches singing and praising God," John continued, and the memory of it put a grim look on his face. "They told me about so many miracles that had happened during the fighting. One Viet Cong threw a hand grenade on the roof of Sau's house. It bounced off, soared right back into the group of guerillas where it had come from, and exploded, killing many enemy soldiers. Since that time the Viet Cong haven't come back to the village, for they are a very superstitious people. They are much more so than the Christian tribespeople. Now they only try to catch individuals when they tend the fields or walk the jungle trails, but the Communists are afraid of this place."

The church filled up long before we entered for the service at which I was to speak. The simple Christmas decorations looked faded, but the bamboo cross in front entwined with evergreens and dried ferns reached straight and unbroken into the deep blue sky. Sau's son, Jimmy, translated my message. I shared with them my own struggle with fear and hate after I had fled a Communist labor camp and how I had found peace and joy when I invited Jesus into my life.

"Your enemies think the way I once thought after being trained by the Nazis," I said through the interpreter. "They believe sincerely that they follow the right cause, but sincerity cannot protect a person from being led astray. Sincerity must be coupled with truth to come to the right end. Don't ever hate those Viet Cong; pray for them. Hate is ugly and big and strong, but we know that love is greater and stronger than hate!"

Hundreds of solemn open faces looked up to me. The children sat quietly, and a deep silence hovered over us and the entire sunbathed village.

Love—greater than hate? Love your enemies? Such words are easily spoken in times of peace and plenty, but they hung heavily in the air when the translator repeated my words in a war-torn village in the Central Highlands of South Vietnam on New Year's Eve of 1974.

It is hard to love a man when he destroys crops that hungry children cry for. It is hard not to hate an enemy whose tactic is to harass and aggravate day in and day out, week after week, year after year. It is hard to go out to the fields and pick up the torn limbs of the father after a hidden mine has exploded under him. It is hard to pray for cruel men who seem to have no heart, compassion, or human sensitivity and who are bent on destruction only. They persecute and torture the innocent and helpless for no other reason than their faith in a God of love.

Many hundreds of deep dark eyes looked earnestly at me without a trace of a smile in their faces.

"I am leaving you a gift," I said to these, my special brothers and sisters in Christ, "something my beloved friend Corrie ten Boom has

taught me. We do not know what the future holds for any of us. I do
not know what is in store for you. If new hardship and danger come,
Satan will try to fill your heart with fear and hate. When that happens,
make a sign of remembrance to yourself and to each other. Take your
thumb and fold it under your four fingers. Clasp the other hand on top
over it and remember: The thumb is you, the four covering fingers are
Christ, and the hand over it is our Father God. Nothing, absolutely
nothing, can ever come to you unless it goes first past the Father and
the Son."

The stony, dark-skinned faces broke into smiles. People nodded; the
native pastor stood up to give the benediction. He prayed for a long time
in the native tongue. At the end he clasped his thumb under his fingers
and laid the other hand over it. We all understood, we all smiled.
Corrie's sign language had reached again more hearts and minds around
the world!

The sun slanted toward the west, and we knew we had to leave soon.
It was not wise to drive the jungle roads after dark. The enemy used the
nights for his dirty work. We took a quick walk through the village while
Jim and some men looked quickly over some fields. The people had
planted new kinds of seed sent to them from America, and they showed
the straight rows of young green sprouts proudly. No more hit-and-miss
planting, as in the days of their forefathers. New methods and fertilizer
brought to them by John produced crops when traditional planting
would have invited more starvation.

John showed "Daddy Jim" the only tractor the village owned. (Jim's
organization had sent it to them.) "Look at the tires," he said.

"What tires?" I said, and couldn't help smiling. It looked comical to
see how the men drove that tractor with the tires hanging in threads
from the wheel hubs.

"We'll ship you tires as soon as I get back to America," Jim promised.
Most of the men didn't understand his words but they knew what he
meant; his nods and smile conveyed the message. They nodded and
smiled back.

Many villagers had gone back to their daily chores after the church
service and singing were over. Men went back to the fields, and women
gathered around the common water trough to wash their laundry. It was

obvious that most of the people's clothing had come from a mission barrel. They washed it without soap, by soaking it in the mountain water piped in by bamboo sticks. Due to the drought, the water only trickled. The women stood in the trough and stomped the wash with their feet. When they felt that it was clean, the wet stuff was draped over fences, bushes, and branches to dry.

Children wandered around naked. One tiny fellow carried a small wood carrier on his back. Even the kids had to help in that struggle for survival, and I watched the very young and the very old carry in sticks and firewood for the evening meal.

We had to leave. Sau had brought some squashes to John as a gift. John knew better than to reject it. The people obviously needed it, but it was unthinkable for those primitive people to let us go without a meal and gifts. Women came to lay strings of colorful little glass beads around our necks. Sau took some slim brass rings out of his pocket. They had been hand-carved by his men and were the most valuable things the tribe possessed. He bent them skillfully to slip them on our right wrists. He looked solemnly up into my face.

"My sister in Christ," he said emphatically, "we give you this bracelet. It will be to you a symbol of Christ's love, which is never ending, like this ring. May it also remind you to tell the American brothers and sisters to pray for us. We need your prayers, we are all alone."

"My brother," I said slowly and very deliberately, "I thank you for this gift. I promise that I shall do what you asked me to do. But remember one thing, you are *never* alone so long as you stay true to God. God and you are a majority!"

The little man nodded. "Yes, we know God's power, and we do love Jesus Christ. But next to Christ, we love him the most," he pointed to John, the American missionary. "He is our greatest and best friend on earth."

I looked at John and at the people. For the first time I realized something. These people, dark-skinned and brown-eyed, short and slim, had an image of Jesus Christ in their loving hearts. They pictured Christ with blue eyes and gray hair, pale-skinned, tall, broad, and rugged. To them Christ looked like an American! He looked like John!

13
Fire in the Mountains

We drove away and I felt dazed. Within twenty-four hours I had gone from the palace of Saigon with all its splendor to the Montagnard tribes, the most primitive people in Vietnam. I had seen a poverty that cannot be described. But who was *really* poor?

In the palace lived a president who always had one foot in the grave. The overthrow of the government was at any moment just one bullet away; and he lived more and more in seclusion and hiding. At least, that was what General Khang confided to me. He should know because his life was as much in jeopardy as the president's. Fear and terror kept the people in high government places in fierce bondage, and they could not enjoy the vain glory of their fancy surroundings.

In the village we had just left, the people would soon gather for the evening services in their four crude bamboo churches. Most of them would still be hungry after the evening meal because corn and rice had to be rationed until the next harvest.

They would sing and praise the Lord and smile. Hadn't God given them another day of peace and quiet and a visit from their beloved friend, John?

If I ever had to choose between those two extremes, I knew where I would go: with the poorest of the poor who had found the riches in Jesus Christ. I'd rather have their peace than the palace's plenty.

"Oh, John," I said and took a deep breath, "what will happen to those beautiful people we just left? What will their future hold?"

"Hansi," John said quietly, "I do not know what their or our future holds, but I know *Who* holds the future. I simply have to believe that something good will happen soon. There has to be an end to all that suffering some day. We missionaries have poured our life and blood into this land for decades. God will honor our work and efforts for Him."

I understood what he meant when I walked into his home in Dalat. It was ever so simple but tastefully arranged. "What a cozy home you have created," I said to Jo, John's wife, who welcomed us warmly.

"Whatever you see in this house has been given to us," she said with a sweet smile. "We have lost everything we owned three times now, and every time when we have come back to our ransacked house, the Lord provided again for all our needs." He not only provided for John's and Jo's needs, he also provided a place of refuge for many others, I noticed.

Sau's oldest sons, John and Jim, who actually had tribal names but preferred to be called by the American names, walked in and out of the mission house as if it were theirs. So did others, and Jo mothered them all.

She mothered me, too, when I needed it. My throat ached and my head throbbed. The dust and hot dryness of the Sut Thong village had not helped my cold a bit, especially since I didn't dare to drink the water they had available. Jo had tea, fruit, and a clean bed for me. The others went to a New Year's Eve service at the tribal center, and I stayed behind for quiet reflection and needed sleep.

The next day I felt much better and enjoyed the beauty of Dalat. What a delightful spot, almost out of place amidst the rugged, wild, dry mountains with its mild climate, pine-scented air, and the abundance of flowers everywhere. We visited several mission places. On the way to them I remarked to John about the many bare hills dotted with tree stumps that I observed.

"It seems to me like the Vietnamese are cutting down their woods everywhere. Aren't they afraid about future erosion and landslides when the rains come?"

John smiled. "Hansi," he said, "have you forgotten how it feels to live without a future? Vietnam has had war for thirty years. People don't plan for their future anymore; they live for today. They sell what they can and spend the money now. Who knows if there is a tomorrow! Japanese firms buy every piece of lumber they can lay their hands on, and the Vietnamese deliver as fast as they can."

I thought of Korea. Would Vietnam end up like South Korea—

treeless, with the topsoil washed away? That would be tragic for the next generation.

One thing I could wish for this bleeding, devastated country—the spreading of the Gospel as it had happened in South Korea. Every indication that it might happen was here. I thought of the many wounded Vietnamese soldiers who had accepted Christ. They felt in need of something solid, something that wouldn't change as did the fate of war and life. They listened so attentively when I spoke through the interpreter to many hundreds of them, and so did many other South Vietnamese. Many listened to the Gospel of love with new ears. But nobody had embraced the message of God's love as the Montagnards had. Sut Thong was only *one* example of the many other tribes of varied dialects through which the Gospel spread like wildfire.

John showed us the language school of the mission. "You know, Hansi," he said in his simple way, "God always fulfills more than one purpose when He does something. He not only used this language school to open the Gospel to more tongues and tribes; He also uses this institution to bring about unity among the various Christian denominations. They forget their petty doctrinal differences as they share the common misery of trying to learn some impossible languages. They have learned to pray together, Catholics and Protestants alike!"

"Are the languages *that* hard?" I asked.

John laughed his dry laugh. "For an American, yes! Some of the tonal dialects consist mainly of consonants, and it's the tone of those consonants that tell you what it means. The Vietnamese language is hard enough, but the many tribal dialects are even harder. Our Bible translators live with the tribes for many years before they can understand and communicate. Then they have to develop a written alphabet and patterns of grammar. After the Bible is translated and printed, they have to teach the tribespeople how to read it."

"Just a minute, John," I said, "are you telling me that Americans who are educated well enough to do such linguistic studies live *with* the tribes for years—in all that primitive dirt and misery?"

"They sure do, kid," he said grimly, "with rats in their huts and cut off from civilization for months at a time. Once in a while they come to the mission center and bring an informer along for further study."

"What is an *informer?*" I asked. The word didn't set too well in my personal frame of reference.

John grinned. "It's a tribal man who comes, often with his whole family. He has learned some English from the translator and is now willing to help the missionary in his research of the tribes' dialects. Sometimes the man has to repeat a word over and over and over again, and the linguist has to look into the fellow's throat with a flashlight to find out how certain sounds are formed. That's how the people in the Sut Thong village got their Bibles; there are three dialects spoken in that one village!"

I made a mental note that I would do a bit more research about the Bible translating work someday.

"The language school was a dream and a baby of mine for a long time," John said. "Whenever one project is done, I promise myself never to start another thing. The headaches and problems are often so frustrating, but I always find something else I *must* do. Come in and see my newest 'baby'!"

We got out of the car and walked into a brand-new hospital. It hadn't opened yet, but it would be ready within short weeks. American generosity had built that place, too. The instruments and appliances bore American trade names, the medicine cabinets were filled with donated medicines from American drug manufacturers.

"The only thing we need urgently now is an X-ray machine," John said and looked at Jim.

"What kind do you need?" Jim asked and pulled out his little notebook.

John gave him data I didn't understand, and Jim wrote it down. "We'll get a used machine to you as soon as I get back to America," Jim promised.

"Whenever we get into a pinch, be it tractor tires, medical equipment or baby food, we contact him," John told me and pointed at Jim. "What would we do out here in the mission field without people in the homeland who are willing to come to our aid and rescue? I tell you it takes teamwork to get the job done!"

Yes, I slowly got a new vision of the kind of teamwork it took to fulfill the commission of Christ.

Some people left their affluence and the homeland behind to become missionaries; others gave their life to serve in the American organizations that backed those people in the field. Behind the organizations stood thousands of people who gave to the cause of missions. And they all did it because they wanted to, by their free will. To someone with my kind of upbringing and training, who had known nothing but outer control, brainwashing, and forced decisions as a youth, it will always be of new amazement to see people do things voluntarily. To think that they do it of their own free will and choice—simply because they want to do it!

"Buildings are important," John said as we walked through the brand-new place, "but I wouldn't have dared to start it if Carol wasn't here."

Carol met us at the hospital. She was the missionary nurse, a single woman in her early thirties, I guessed. She radiated a quiet warmth and tranquility that I admire so deeply in people.

"Doctors come and go on short-term mission service," John continued, "but Carol stays and keeps our medical work going, year in, year out."

"This is my life," Carol said simply and motioned around her, "I live for it."

"Do you plan to stay here all your life?" someone in the group asked.

"Yes, if that is God's will," she said and smiled. I looked at her. She was attractive, educated, dependable, and of sweet disposition. She had every right in the world to ask for her own slice of the American pie— a husband, a family, affluent living in the land she had been lucky enough to be born in. Instead, she chose to help primitive tribespeople in endless hours of medical service.

"We nearly lost her a while ago," John told me later when Carol wasn't around. "You have no idea how *hard* it is to be a single woman in the mission field. The natives treat a woman without a husband with contempt. She is misunderstood, attacked by gossip, left out, and the missionary families can often be as thoughtless and cruel as the heathen. But I tell you, I *dared* to build this hospital because that girl has a backbone of steel!"

"John, where is the kitchen?" I asked before we left the hospital. "You have everything else—rooms for surgery and other treatment, Carol's place where she receives people and hands out medicines, the wards—but don't people have to eat?"

"Yes, they do, but we don't feed them; their families do. A patient never comes alone; sometimes the whole clan will camp around our medical facilities. The family cooks between a few rocks or whatever they can find." John led us to the back of the building.

"We do have a cooking place with ten cooking spots all prepared at the end of the building; all the patients' families need to bring now are the wood, the pot, and the rice. The little fireplaces are ready! This is our kitchen." John sounded so proud. I pictured the glistening white and stainless steel kitchens of even the smallest American hospital and smiled.

We left the hospital and drove back to John's house. Part of our group stayed in a doctor's home. It's a chore to house and feed eight people even when conditions are ideal, but it's hard for people in the mission field to give hospitality to American visitors. We Americans are so spoiled, even in such small luxuries like toilet paper, napkins, the wasting of too many towels and hot water. We take things for granted that are luxuries, to be used sparingly, by our dear missionaries.

One luxury that Jo had, which we don't have in America, is servants. Every missionary family I met in the Orient had one or more servants. Maybe they are not a luxury but a necessity. They go to the daily market to buy fresh vegetables and native foods. If the missionary wife had to do it, her budget would suffer more than if she paid a servant. Labor is cheap and so are market prices until a foreigner tries to buy something. It takes years to learn the art of bargaining and haggling. The natives are masters in it, so Jo's cook goes to the market. Then she soaks the vegetables in bleach water and disinfects everything that is prepared for a meal. She washes sheets, towels, and table linen laboriously by hand. All these manual chores take hours in a primitive society, and if Jo did them herself she wouldn't have time to do what she had come for: to teach people about the Gospel.

"Servants can be a headache," Jo said. "It takes a year to train them and teach them enough of our language to be able to communicate. Very often, after they are trained, they are bribed with higher pay to leave and go where the grass is greener—which means that I have to start all over!

"On the other hand, every servant is a mission prospect. We share the Gospel with them. Very often, after they accept it, they will help convert their whole family. Right now I feel very lucky. My cook is very devoted to us. I know she has been offered much higher pay several times, but the woman will not leave us. She is fiercely protective and loyal to us and has been with us for years!"

The servant had set the table the American way and waited in the kitchen for Jo's signals. Jo had outdone herself in giving us the best she had to offer. The meal was delicious. She had opened some cans from America, too. It was a luxury she saved for special occasions. I was mostly interested in the fresh salad.

"It is safe to eat it, Hansi," she said. "My cook is very dependable. It's soaked for hours in various solutions to destroy the parasites!" I ate it with gusto although it had a slight taste of bleach and other chemicals. I missed fresh salad the most on the tour.

"John," I said while we ate, "this whole Vietnam thing puzzles me no end. I am not very knowledgeable when it comes to politics, but can you explain to me why America lost the war in Vietnam? It's so hard for me to understand why the greatest, strongest nation on this globe got licked by a few rice farmers. That's what it amounted to, when the American soldiers pulled out, didn't it?"

John gave me a long, silent look. "Let me tell you something," John said very slowly. "The American soldiers didn't lose the war, the American news media did. For one or the other reason someone decided that Vietnam wasn't worth saving. Even while our men were sent over here to fight, they were told from the beginning that they didn't come to win a war. I tell you, what our boys did *in spite* of such demoralizing orders and attitudes will someday go down in history in a way different from the way the American press of today wishes to portray it. Do you remember when we came yesterday around that sharp bend where the bridge is just a makeshift?"

I nodded. Sure, I held my breath while we crossed over that flimsy thing!

"I sat at the end of the road one day while the Americans were still fighting together with the South Vietnamese and watched something," John continued. "I tell you, our air force especially is something to behold. A few American Marines had gone with some South Vietnamese soldiers on patrol up on the mountain top right above that bridge. Suddenly they encountered a nest of Viet Cong and were trapped. They exchanged fire, but the VCs were too strong. I watched the whole thing through my binoculars. The Americans sent a wireless message and just dug in and waited. Within minutes several American airplanes appeared out of nowhere and attacked the guerrillas. They didn't miss by a yard. They cleaned the nest out without so much as giving one scratch to our boys. There is no better air force than ours!" John sounded proud and troubled at the same time. "The American press has deliberately smeared our boys and made them a bunch of dope-takers, rapists, and scoundrels. Listen, they were not all bad. We had some rotten eggs. Aren't they everywhere? But they got all the headlines and the decent, fine kids who came over here are never talked about."

"Well, what about the massacre of My Lai?" I said. "That really shook all of America up!"

"Let me say this much," John said thoughtfully. "You know I don't believe in hate, revenge, and killing. I am a minister of the Gospel, and I came to this land to heal, not to hurt. But I wish the American press had been fair enough to present both sides of that story, too, and let the American public make up their own mind about it.

"You see, some villages here in South Vietnam have collaborated completely with the Viet Cong. The village of My Lai was in the war zone, and people had been *told* to leave. They didn't and became totally loyal to the Communist side instead. I don't know why, whether they had been brainwashed, were forced, or were doing it by free will. The fact remains that we missionaries had been told *never* to go near that village, for they killed anything in sight that wasn't Communistic. War is a dirty business, and it isn't played by fair rules when Communists fight. They make an enemy out of women and children! They sent a five-year-old child over to the Americans to beg for gum. When our boys gave it to him, the child exploded, for under his shirt he carried several sticks of dynamite tied to his waist. The child and the whole group of GIs were killed.

"Hansi," John said with a catch in his voice, "our boys had lost more than eighty of their buddies because of that village, and you forget to worry if it is a child or a woman. If they try to kill you, it's an enemy and it is either your life or theirs. I don't have all the answers but I know one thing: the story was as slanted as anything else the news says about this land. It makes me angry!"

"John, what bothers me the most is what a young American woman said to me just recently. She said, 'I am raising three little boys alone because my husband had to die in that miserable Vietnam war—for nothing!' "

"Don't ever say that," John said, and he raised his voice. "Don't let anybody say that our American boys died for *nothing* anywhere. The Gospel of Jesus Christ is spreading here in Vietnam as it has never before, and God uses everything to do His purpose, even this war. Yes, our boys died over here, but thousands of Vietnamese people will live forever in God's kingdom because of it."

I didn't answer. My tears spilled into my food. God, I thought, I wish I could repeat what John has said to all those American mothers, fathers, and wives who had lost their loved ones during the war. Here I sit, a Christian and an American by choice because America helped to win World War II to liberate what was brainwashed and oppressed in Europe. South Korea is the most Christian nation on the globe because America preserved for them their freedom of worship; Vietnam is turning more and more to the God of love—and the Americans are told that their sons died for *nothing?*

"Did anybody ever tell you about the revival that has swept through these Central Highlands the past few years?" John asked, and he sounded as though he was ready to take on all those who always tell only *one* side of the story. "Listen carefully. That revival was started by young GIs of the American Jesus movement. In their spare time they would go to the beaches and the streets of Saigon and hand out Christian literature. Their shiny faces and big smiles attracted the Vietnamese people. Some native students of the mission school in Saigon became acquainted with them and dragged them into the school so they could give their testimony. Our American boys shared the spiritual fire in their hearts and it began a revival in that school. The native students picked up the torch and carried it to the people. The tribal boys went home and shared the new things they had seen and heard—and revival swept from tribe to tribe."

"Did that happen just recently?" I asked.

"In just the last few years and the results are overwhelming!" John nodded.

"When it hit the Sut Thong village the people stayed for three days and nights in their churches to sing and pray," Jo interrupted. "They confessed their sins to each other and made wrongs right. Because the VCs hadn't attacked so much lately, they had become less fervent in their faith. Gossip and tension sneak in so easily anywhere. Some women were not even speaking to each other any more. But when the revival hit, that former spirit of brotherhood got rekindled, and they had a big spiritual clean-up!"

"They had more than that," John said. "Some sick were healed, one mountain tribe reports even a dead man raised back to life. If that was so or not may be questioned, but God set the mountains on fire. Those people are still burning for Him!

"Speaking of fire," he continued, "when it happened at Sut Thong and our people finally went out to their fields and back to their daily routine, people of neighboring villages came and asked our people if the fire had done great damage to the village.

" 'What fire?' the Sut Thong people asked their neighbors.

" 'We have seen the bright shine of a big fire for the last three nights over your village.' the heathen said. 'We wondered if your village was burning to the ground!' "

No, the village hadn't burned away! Only the love for God and each other had been rekindled, and the fire of that love still burned to warm our hearts on New Year's Day of 1975.

14
Will We See Them Again?

Time to leave again! We made our way to the airport in plenty of time to board the old propeller plane scheduled for Saigon. At least we hoped we would get there! Plane schedules in Vietnam were subject to change even at the last moment, as we knew by then from experience. Sure enough, the flight was delayed for two hours. Nobody complained; it simply was a way of life. As long as a plane could leave at all, why fuss?

John and Jo stayed with us to make sure we really got away safely. I sat in silence. The last two days had done something to me! I knew I'd never be the same again.

"Hansi," John said, "you're so quiet, what's eating you?"

"Nothing," I smiled, "I just can't stop thinking about all the things I saw and heard up here in the Central Highlands, and how our American boys set the spark for the new revival!"

I didn't tell John that I felt an uneasiness about it deep in my heart. I remembered what someone had told me in Korea. Big revivals had preceded the Communist invasions first in the North and then in South Korea. Revivals had prepared the Korean Christians for persecution, suffering, and death.

"Talking about the beginning of the revival among the tribespeople," Jo interrupted my thinking, "God has a wonderful way of closing a circle, Hansi! Americans began it, but on the other hand, God used some of the simple mountain people to lead some Americans back to God in return.

"Just before the Americans pulled out, one of the highest-ranking American officers in Dalat had a talk with one of Sau's sons. The boy told him about Jesus, and shared with the officer how to accept the Lord. That well-known, highly decorated American man was humble enough to let himself be led to Christ by a native, tribal boy. He accepted Christ on the spot. Two days later his helicopter crashed and he was killed."

"The tribespeople do a lot more preaching than they dream of," Jim said quietly. "Ever since *The Bamboo Cross* by Homer F. Dowdy was published in 1964, thousands of Americans have been affected by its contents. That book is powerful!"

"Isn't God doing what He always does?" Cathy, our black sister, asked. "He chooses the weak, the despised, and those the world considers foolish and of little value to glorify His name. Praise the Lord!" Cathy was the gospel singer of our group, and the Sut Thong people had loved her singing and her contagious big smile. We loved it, too. She could brighten the most tense moments of our travel with her expressions of joy in the Lord, and people just loved to be around her.

"We hate to see you all go," Joe said a bit wistfully. "Visits like yours stay with us for a long time."

I thought of Harriet in Seoul and what she had said when we left. I realized again that missionaries missed what those of us back home take so much for granted: Christian fellowship and social interaction in our American churches.

For thousands of tribal people, John is a father figure and Jo a mother. The "God-followers" look to them for leadership, help, trouble shooting, and the portrayal of Jesus Christ. Missionaries are expected to give and give and give. What happens when *they* need refilling and the restoration that comes out of Christian fellowship among their own people? No wonder they cherish visitors so much!

I hated to leave, but we finally had to climb into that rickety plane and fly off back to the smelly traffic and the congestion of late afternoon traffic in Saigon!

Don and Jim had planned a birthday reception for the legendary Madame Le. It was to be held on a boat the Vietnamese had changed into a fancy restaurant. I liked her from the moment she arrived in a beautiful native *áo-dài*. I had been briefed about her before we met. Her husband, a Vietnamese general, had been next in line to be president until he died ten years ago. Madame Le had four children by her husband. Then, when her brother was killed, she adopted *his* four children and on top of that she adopted four more war orphans. That's unheard of in a society that ignores widows and orphans as worthless. So she had twelve children and very little money, and she started a pig farm.

When we met her, she was a wealthy woman again, who worked closely with American organizations to relieve the suffering of her people. One of the baby homes we had visited the week before had been one of her own large homes. She had given it to Jim's organization. Her pig farm also employed many war widows, and she acted as the national president of the new Women's Association.

Here sat another slim, tiny woman with very tall bearing and a stoic dignity. I wondered if she had any uncontrolled emotions, ever! She acted so poised, self-assured, and strong. She spoke a simple English very rapidly.

"When you come back to Vietnam," she said it almost like giving an order, "you *must* be my personal guest. I will show you my pig farm and introduce you to my women's work. That is, if you *can* come back. You see, the next offensive is coming very soon, I know it!

"You see," she continued without blinking an eye, "my servants love me and they always tell me: Madame, don't leave your house on such and such time or day. They know what is coming. A very big fight is coming! What can I do but die with my people?"

"Madame Le," I said slowly, "to die for the sake of dying helps nobody. Do you believe in God?"

"I am a Buddhist," she said a bit defensively.

"Madame Le, I shall pray to *my* God and ask Him to protect you and to keep you alive for your twelve children!"

I wondered if I saw moisture well up into her eyes, but in the dim twilight of the lanterns I couldn't be sure. I looked over the dark river and watched the stars shimmer. What could I *say* to such a woman that would leave hope and peace with her? I looked at Cathy, our dark nightingale.

"Cathy, please sing for Madame Le before we leave. Sing 'our' song: 'Because He lives, I can face tomorrow'—please!"

Cathy hesitated. We sat on the deck of a fancy restaurant-boat amidst

Orientals. Everybody behaved as was the custom—very quiet, subdued, inconspicuous. The cool moist night air made Cathy cough. But she nodded and stood up. "Madame," she said, "as my birthday gift to you I would like to sing a song."

Cathy flipped the button of her little cassette recorder for the accompaniment and then her beautiful voice rang out in a Bill Gaither song:

> Because He lives, I can face tomorrow;
> Because He lives, all fear is gone;
> Because I know He holds the future.
> And life is worth the living
> Just because He lives!

A deep hush lingered when Cathy finished.

Don cleared his throat.

"Madame Le, in deepest appreciation for all your help and cooperation with our childcare program and everything else you have done, we would like to present to you a leather-bound Bible with your name engraved on it in gold letters. And now: Happy Birthday and many blessed returns!"

We all clapped and sang, "Happy Birthday."

Madame Le held the Bible in her hand and said, visibly moved, "I will read it."

I hugged her when she left and said again: "Remember, I *will* pray for you and your children!"

She nodded, "Yes, you pray for me. I need it!"

The next morning she met us for breakfast at the Saigon airport. We were leaving Vietnam to fly into Cambodia.

She saw to it that we had breakfast the American way—with eggs, rolls, and fruit. I watched her flip her fingers and give orders. The waiters knew her and tried very much to please her. It was obvious that the woman was highly respected and loved by her people.

General Khang and his wife had come to see us off, too. He wore his uniform.

"I don't like you in uniform, General," I teased him. "I am allergic to soldiers and war!"

"Hansi," he said, "I am *not* a soldier, I am a marine, partially trained in the United States, remember that!"

"Oh, dear, what an insult," I grinned at him.

"I read your entire book last night," the general said. "It gave me great insights. I liked it very much!"

"Thank you," I said, and thought: "Did you like my Jesus, too?"

I knew they were Buddhists, but George and Virginia, who had been guests in the general's house, had told me that they saw an open Bible beside the general's bed.

The time to board the Cambodian aircraft had come. A special foreboding seemed to move over all of us. American missionaries, Don, our Vietnamese friends—they all had come to see us off—and tears flowed on both sides.

Mrs. Khang sobbed when she hugged me. "Please pray for us, we do not know what will happen to us!"

Did she know something we didn't know, I wondered.

I said good-bye to everyone, then I turned to look for Madame Le. She sat by herself on a bench and wasn't aware that I looked at her. Her face showed such forlorn pain and sadness that I went over and kissed her on her cheek.

"Remember that I am your sister," I said. "I care deeply about you and my God *will* protect you and keep you!"

Her eyes filled with tears. "Please come back and be *my* guest next time," she said urgently.

"I promise," I smiled through tears, "and," fumbling in my bag, "here is my card with my address. The second telephone number on it is my private number. Should you ever come to the United States, please let me know. I want to see you!"

We walked through the gate and everybody waved. Something choked me, a great concern, a presentiment, a deep loving care for all these dear people we were leaving behind.

"God, will we see them again?" I prayed silently. "Please keep them in the hollow of Your hand. Please, God, they are all so very special— protect them."

I recalled what John had said, "Hansi, I *have* to believe that something good will happen."

"God," I said, "the Gospel is spreading through South Vietnam. Don't let the Communists stop it. Let this land become another South Korea, if it is in Your will. Oh, God, let me see those precious people again!"

15
Simon and Thunder

The Cambodian aircraft circled over Phnom Penh and then took a straight dive down. The sudden change in altitude added to the discomfort of a cramped seat and an overfilled plane, and my stomach churned again.

"These Cambodian pilots need to be taught how to land right," I thought and remembered the hundreds of smooth landings in America I had taken for granted! The plane hit the ground roughly but finally bounced to a standstill. We squeezed ourselves out and down the wobbly steps and hurried to get to customs before the long lines formed.

Jim looked puzzled. He glanced around and searched every face.

"It is strange," he said. "I have a very dear friend in the Cambodian government. He is one of the top officials. He has always been here to welcome me before and see to it that customs didn't give me any trouble. I did write to him to tell him of our arrival, but I can't see him anywhere!"

Customs turned out to be easier than expected in spite of the Cambodian's absence, and we soon walked out of the terminal building. An American missionary welcomed us with a broad grin and began to pile our luggage into the back of a van. I looked around. A deep blue sky spanned over us without a single cloud; the sun shone brightly on a deep green land. The native people moved around without hurry, and I should have enjoyed the obvious tranquility—but something bothered me! What was it?

There was a strange noise in the air, a noise I had heard before. It sounded like thunder, faraway continuous thunder. But that couldn't be! The sky had no thunderclouds!

We piled on top of our luggage in the vehicle and drove off. I didn't talk much. I listened. The thunder-like noise seemed to increase, and suddenly I knew what it was. This wasn't thunder, these were detonations—the roar of war! For many peaceful years in America I hadn't had any reason to remember the sounds of war, but I still could recognize war booms when I heard them.

The car stopped in front of a mission guest house. The gates opened. I walked into the house and looked into the smiling face of the missionary's wife. She appeared tired but very friendly.

"Welcome to Cambodia," she said.

"Are these war sounds?" I interrupted her while I nodded toward the door that seemed to vibrate continuously under the noise of nearby explosions.

She nodded. "Oh, yes," she said. "I am very surprised that you even came!"

"Nobody told us that we were flying into the midst of war," I said and looked for Jim. He wasn't around, but I was sure that he hadn't known either. He was too responsible a man to take us without our consent into a risky situation like this.

"I believe it," our hostess continued. "The Cambodian radio hasn't even mentioned the new offensive yet. It started three nights ago, and it is the worst I have ever heard. The shooting hasn't stopped once for the last three days and nights."

I knew now why she looked so tired. How could anyone sleep in this banging and rumbling?

"It sounds very near," I said. "How close are we to the actual fighting line?"

She shrugged nonchalantly and said, "Give or take three blocks. It's just on the other side of the river. The rockets are coming across the river constantly. A little home across the street from us got hit last night; we could hear them cry. Some of the people were killed and others wounded."

"You sound so matter-of-fact about it all," I smiled a bit. "Aren't you concerned?"

"We are so used to it by now," she said wearily. "War and offensives have been part of Cambodia for so long. It comes and goes like the dry and rainy season. We have learned to take it in stride and wait. It will go away again as soon as the rains come—and God is with us!"

God is with us! I nodded and felt myself relax to the tasks at hand.

"First of all we need to put Ann to bed," I said. "She got sick before we left Saigon and refused to admit it. The flight didn't help too much. She looks ready to drop!"

Ann protested feebly, but we got her into a bed. A servant brought boiled, cool water, and we turned the fan on. The air felt stifling, and a strange smell hung over the land. Oh, how I hated the smell of explosives!

Then I found Jim and asked what the plans were. Our itinerary showed five days of visiting in Cambodia.

"Jim, Ann is too sick to stay that long," I said. "She will not be able to rest too much with all this noise; how soon can we get out again?"

"The next plane leaves in two days," Jim said, "and we will make reservations at once. If it is God's will, we get to Thailand by Friday night!"

I nodded. God had a reason for keeping us in Cambodia for two days, I was sure of that, and I was eager to find out why.

Our first visit took us to the Nutrition Center. I didn't know what a Nutrition Center was and was in no way prepared for what I had to see.

It was a home for sick and malnourished babies and was stuffed full. Some cribs contained two or more of those little things that resembled babies, and the air was thick with the mixed smells of urine, disinfectants, and the body odor of the many natives who hovered around almost every crib. I knew by then that in the Orient a patient never stays isolated from his or her family. The babies had either their mother or a grandmother or some other relative close by. It made the overcrowded condition in that small building even more difficult. And hygiene was nearly impossible.

Sandra, an Australian nurse, was in charge of the center. She looked tired but appeared very calm and treated us ever so graciously.

"Are all these Cambodians around the cribs of any help to you?" I asked her.

"Only so far as we can teach them how to take care of their babies after we release the child," she said in her Australian accent. "These mothers are so ignorant about the most basic principles of childcare that we often win a battle for a baby after long weeks here in the hospital only to see the child die later anyway when the mother takes it back!"

"Do all these poor things have parents?" I asked, because some cribs had nobody close by except occasionally a nurse or a native nurse's aide.

"I wish they did," Sandra sighed. "We always have between twenty and thirty little orphans around, too. I can't wait until the new American children's hospital opens. They'll be so much better equipped to look after the very sick babies. The orphans are so often our worst cases because they were neglected the most after the parents abandoned them or were killed."

She moved a baby blanket back and pointed at a little form. "We just got him in. He is one of our orphans. We do not know if we can save him; he isn't responding or gaining weight yet."

I had to force myself to keep looking. What I saw was too much for tears. Sure, I had seen pictures of such babies before, but not until I saw one with my own eyes did I believe that such little figures really existed. The tiny face looked grotesquely shriveled and old, the closed eyelids fluttered weakly, the arms and legs stuck out like thin bamboo sticks from a drum—the skin was that tightly drawn over protruding ribs and bloated tummy—the whimper was more surmised than heard. The spark of life was giving a last flicker. Would they be able to fan it back to life or would it go out?

I swallowed hard. "How do you know when the babies are sick and what is wrong with them?"

"We don't," Sandra said grimly. "We have a missionary doctor come in to help us as much as possible, but most of the time we just make educated guesses. When the measles hit, they die by the dozens. TB we can guess at when they are weighed. If a baby doesn't gain at all, we have a good reason to believe that it has tuberculosis."

"Do you keep the TB-infected babies separated from the others who gain weight?" I asked.

"How?" she said with a weary sweep of her arm to take the whole situation in. "How can we? We are so overfilled now, and the babies keep coming in from the fighting areas. We can't just turn them away.

We'll have a better chance to save more of them when the new hospital opens—it's just a question of a few more weeks."

I stood and took it all in: the many flies that crawled over little faces, the thin wails of babies who were too weak to cry loud, the hot, sticky air full of pungent smells, and the noise of war coming through the glassless screened windows, while young white women were going around and giving of themselves amidst the misery—helping, healing, nursing, and smiling!

It felt good to see Sandra from Australia as a part of the American team who worked in the Nutrition Center. It seemed so important to me to bring other nationalities into the program of helping. The United States carries *most* of the load, but it can't do it alone anymore. There is too much to do—everywhere!

The rest of our American group were still looking and taking pictures when I walked outside. I had to get some fresh air and needed to control my emotions. Suffering gets to me at any level, but I had never seen so many tiny lives wasting away before they had a chance to be.

I watched some healthy-looking toddlers playing in the sandbox. Native nurses' aides looked after them. A young American girl stopped beside me and said, "These are mostly orphans. We have had them long enough to bring them back to normalcy. It is amazing what a good milk formula, vitamins, and love can do for such children!"

The look of the smiling lively children lifted my spirits. I walked over and began to hand out candies.

Sandra came through a door with a healthy, plump baby in her arm. "See this boy? When he came to us, he looked just like the one I showed you in there. We battled hard for his life. We fed him every half hour with a few drops of formula around the clock for many weeks—look at him now!" I looked into that young woman's face. Her voice carried more than professional pride and satisfaction. Here spoke a young mother.

"Is that *your* baby?" I asked and knew the answer already.

"Yes," she beamed, "the papers just came through. He is mine by adoption and his name is Simon!"

"He looks like you," I smiled and everybody laughed.

Simon had dark Polynesian skin, brown eyes, and black curly hair. The new mother was reddish-blond, very fair-skinned, and blue-eyed. What did it matter?

Although she had not given birth to him, he had become a part of her in endless long night hours when she had struggled to keep him alive. He knew nothing about that; all he knew was that life was great—and he gurgled, grabbed for his mother's hair, and cuddled up to her.

I wanted the same for every orphan in the sandbox and in the cribs so very much that my heart ached some more. I pointed at the playing children. "How much chance is there that we can find parents for all these orphans?" I asked.

"We are working on it," Sandra said. "The Cambodian government hesitates to let them go, but we keep on hoping."

"If the war gets worse, who will take care of them in case you have to leave?" I asked.

"We intend to stay," Sandra said seriously. "If we are forced to leave, we hope to take the children with us if at all possible. But if not, we have trained enough natives to take over!"

"You should be allowed to take them with you; after all, they are yours in more than one way. You saved their lives, you'd stick it out here in the midst of danger, war, and misery for those kids' sake. I admire your unselfishness and dedication so very much," I said, deeply moved.

"Don't admire us," the nurse said. "We often feel so inadequate when baby after baby dies. We just try to do what our Lord told us to do, and He gives us the strength and help we need."

I hugged her and her little baby boy and turned to leave.

"God," I prayed silently, "look after this place and all these little kids, but look out especially for the orphans. Please give them a fair chance just like little Simon has—and like I had! Give them someone special to love and to belong to—and may they live to know You, the giver of life and love."

We hurried to the car. Dusk began to fall, and we knew that we had to return to the mission house at once. The Cambodian government enforced a curfew from sunset to sunrise, and the city reminded me of a ghost town as we sped back to our quarters.

The war noises seemed to intensify and get louder and uglier as the night darkened—but perhaps it was only my own imagination. Maybe my nerves were raw because I couldn't forget the sights I had just seen. Maybe the shooting would stop soon.

Somewhere I heard a child scream, frightened, shrill, a continuous wail. Oh, God, I thought, when will the thunder stop? Little Simon, are you asleep in spite of it?

The group was greeted in Korea with smiles of welcome, armfuls of red carnations and a friendliness which warmed the "mild" winter. *Left:* Hansi at the Yung Nak Church in Seoul, Korea, an "especially reverenced" house of worship started by a handful of Christians who had fled persecution in the North.

Korean orphans who seemed to say, "Take me home. I need a mommy."

Hansi and one of the blind Korean orphans who "sing like angels."

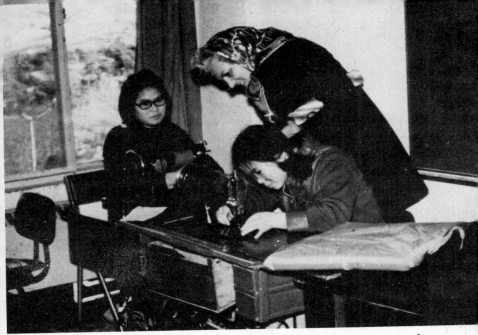

Vocational training for Korean orphans is an attempt to prepare them for adult life in their unsettled country. *Below:* Hansi with some of the "true Americans" in Formosa (Taiwan), the next stop after Korea.

Struggling with chopsticks. Shown with author is gospel singer, Cathy. " . . . our black sister. She could brighten the most tense moments of our travels." *Below:* Distributing candies to orphans. "We never went anywhere without big bags of candies, but we never had enough!"

A peaceful haven in their war-torn world. "But when will the thunder stop?" *Below:* "There were so many that nobody bothered to count them anymore." One of the many refugee groups which author visited on her travels.

A Far East baby home. "God, please give them someone special to love and belong to . . . ." *Below:* Jimmy's (and now Hansi's) Angel's Christian Orphanage. " . . . held together by the blood of Jesus Christ."

Jimmy in his Cambodian orphanage. "He filled his house to the brim with children." *Below:* Jimmy and his new orphan work at the Thai border: Wat Pak Got Camp near Cambodia.

Author with her Nigerian hairdresser. A ten-dollar beauty treatment for Hansi's "impossible, straight hair." *Below:* Orphans in Korea—Hansi's favorite picture. "It's up to the *true* Americans. May God wake us all up before it is too late."

16
It's Spreading Like Wildfire

The shooting didn't stop, it did not even lessen in the wee morning hours, and I lay wide awake on my sagging mattress and tried not to toss. Ann seemed to be asleep. I didn't want to wake her up, she had been so sick and feverish—too sick to eat or to get up.

After a cold shower in a most simple setting the next morning, the bell called us for breakfast. The Cambodian maid who served us had a tear-stained face.

"This woman has lost three members of her family in the last few weeks," the missionary lady said. "Yesterday her nephew stood with a group of young people on the bank of the river, not very far from here, and a rocket exploded in their midst, killing the boy."

"Is she a Christian?" I asked, thinking of how much easier it could make it for her if she knew the comforting presence and love of Jesus in such dark moments.

"We always share our hope with them," the housemother said quietly. "Only God knows what's in their hearts."

Eugene, the missionary who sat at the head of the long table across from his wife, opened a devotional book for morning worship. Around him sat his four children, ranging from eight years of age into various teen ages. We all sat silently and listened as he read. Once in a while a sharp cracking sound interrupted the steady rumbling from the river. We newcomers knew by now that exploding rockets gave a sound similar to our American firecrackers on the Fourth of July. Only these rockets were not meant to celebrate but to kill.

When Gene laid the book down, he looked at me.

"Hansi," he said and his kind, clean face seemed to shine with an inner glow, "what we have been waiting for is finally happening!"

I frowned. "What do you mean? Have you been waiting for this new offensive?"

"No, I don't mean that," Eugene smiled. "We don't need to wait for the offensive. They have come and gone as regularly as the dry and rainy seasons for years. But with this heavy fighting has come what we prayed and waited for—the Gospel of Jesus Christ is spreading like wildfire through Cambodia."

"Why is that?" someone asked.

"The suffering has multiplied so much," Eugene said softly, "that Buddhism has no more answers for the mourning families. Jesus Christ does—and the people are streaming into our church services. Buildings cannot hold them any longer, so we just find a fairly safe grassy spot anywhere and gather the people together under the blue sky. We instruct them as fast as possible, and we are adding hundreds of new believers every week!"

"It's the educated and professional people who show the greatest interest," a preacher from Canada, who also stayed at the guesthouse with us, interrupted Eugene. "I am giving right now a special seminar in lay witnessing and preaching, and the classes are filled with lawyers, doctors, businessmen, and government officials."

"We must teach them fast and only the great Bible essentials," Eugene said, and I noticed again the same deep urgency in his voice I had noticed before in the voices of other missionaries in other lands of the Orient.

"I praise God that the Word is spreading," I said to Eugene, "but tell me, what will happen if the war gets so bad that you missionaries have to leave? After all, these believers are just babes in Christ, they need. . . ."

"We'll *never* leave," Eugene interrupted me and his voice rose, "never, unless they force us! And if they make us leave, we'll come back. It has happened before and might happen again, but we will never leave our Cambodian believers. They need us! I am sure the embassy will demand that the children are sent out within the next few days and we shall do it. We have done it before. But we grown-ups will stay! The children might have to go back early to their school in Malaysia!"

"Do you send *all* of them to boarding school?" I asked and looked at their little girl who wasn't past primary school age.

"Our children leave for boarding school at the age of six," the mother said gently.

"Then you have to do what the missionaries in Vietnam are doing," I said, shocked. "How hard it must be for all of you!"

"It's fun to go to school where my brothers go," the little girl smiled at me and wiggled. She waited for the prayer so we could begin eating.

Eugene prayed and we all ate in silence.

"Why do people have to wait for war and suffering before they open their hearts to Christ?" Cathy, our black singer, spoke and looked at Eugene.

"Buddhism is extremely family-centered and built on ancestor worship. People in years past had a hard time leaving their family unit to follow Christ. The war is destroying that unit, and people have nothing to fall back on. Their only security is gone, and they reach eagerly for 'the Rock' that cannot break. Everything else is breaking!"

Yes, everything else was broken or breaking from day to day. We could clearly see that as we went down to the banks of the river to take a closer look at the fighting line on the other side of the water. It was the end of the dry season, and the riverbanks had shrunk close together; one could see the fighting without binoculars. A big boat, broken down and burning, was sinking slowly like a captive giant in the middle of the water. The earth convulsed and ripped open wherever the grenades hit. It was obvious that the Communists had more material and manpower. The Cambodians fought a losing battle for their freedom, that much could be seen.

"I want to go over there and help those poor Cambodians," Jim said, and I watched the big knuckles of his clenched hands turn white. His blue eyes turned dark with intense emotions, and his face looked grim and hot. I looked up to him and had to smile a bit. Cathy called him "the great white father." It wasn't his white hair alone that gave him a father image. Under that tall, wide, rugged frame did beat a big, warm heart for the needs of the whole suffering world. When people needed food or milk powder or an X-ray machine, Jim knew what to do. When fanatical Communists of a neighboring country break into a land and slaughter everyone who is not willing to think their way, Jim feels helpless and frustrated. I understood how he felt. I would have felt the same way if I had been born in America as he was, but I wasn't.

Because of my different background I felt different, so different that it surprised me. Not until I stood on the riverbank of the Mekong River that early January morning in 1975 did I know how much Jesus Christ had changed that former Nazi girl, Hansi. I felt no hate and most of all no fear anymore!

Yes, men of similar ideology had treated me cruelly after World War II in a Communist slave labor camp. For years after I escaped from it, I hated my torturers and shook in fear whenever anything reminded me of war or violence. Jesus took my hate and fears away; slowly and patiently He changed me—but I didn't know how much He had turned me around until I came face to face with Communists and raw ugly war again. I ached inside but not because I was afraid or I longed to go and fight them. I ached in deep compassion for the losing Cambodians. I wondered how many knew Christ before they had to die?

For the Communists I felt a deeper ache. Yes, many of them died, too—but how much chance did *any* of them have to know about Jesus? Brainwashed, misguided for a supposedly great cause, they probably believed as sincerely as I once did that they followed the right stars. And they died as my Nazi friends did—believing a lie!

How was it that I had been permitted to find Truth—and that Truth had set me free? Yes, free from hate, bitterness, desire for revenge, and the fears of death. I watched people die across from me on the riverbank, hating and destroying each other although they had never had a chance to decide for themselves if that's what they really wanted. One group was as shackled and bound as the other—and I stood there and prayed for the men on both sides, and for their women and children.

I was told that the families stayed with their fighting husband and father. That's why whole families were often partially or altogether wiped out. Because the Communists were winning most of the battles, more and more women and children fled the fighting lines and tried to paddle across the river. These refugee rafts became a favorite target for the Reds. By sinking the women and children, they demoralized and broke the spirit of the Cambodian soldiers.

In spite of the many who drowned, Phnom Penh seemed to become slowly one gigantic refugee camp. We visited the one at the Cambodiana, a huge half-finished complex of cement and steel that had been planned to be Cambodia's largest and fanciest hotel some day—and mainly for Western visitors.

The abandoned project was now used as a crude shelter for hundreds and perhaps thousands of refugees—nobody bothered to count them anymore! Why should they?

The people hovered under anything that gave some shade from the bright, hot sun and they smiled at us. Stark naked children came toward us and shouted a cheery "Hi!" My fingers itched. I had candies in my pockets but I knew better than to begin handing them out. I would get through the first few dozens and then look at hundreds of outstretched, empty little hands. I couldn't bear the thought and kept the few candies I still carried from the day before.

"What a friendly, open, warm people the Cambodians are," I remarked to Jim. "Look at us, here we come: well dressed, well fed, with big photo lenses and empty hands—and everybody smiles at us, waves, poses for pictures, and I can't see a trace of resentment or hostility anywhere!"

"The Cambodians are a Polynesian kind of people, similar to the Hawaiians, very childlike and friendly and very fond of the Americans," Jim said. "I wish people in America could see what we see. They'd change their minds about Vietnam and Cambodia!"

I nodded but didn't answer. Americans can be very thoughtless, but they are seldom heartless, I thought. It's just that the news media didn't give them the true picture of what was happening over here. I knew that Jim felt that the American news media was deliberately giving distorted reports on Southeast Asia, but it was hard for me to accept that. Communist presses would do such a thing but not the free press of my beloved homeland, the United States of America.

We got back into the car and drove up north on one of the main streets beside the river. We stopped to watch refugees stream up the bank; several rafts had made it safely across. Women carried children, a few belongings, a little sack of rice, or sometimes nothing. Some had obviously gotten away to save their own skin only! Here they climbed up rejoicing that they had made it to safety—but for how long?

Rockets exploded here and there in the city, and the food supplies had dwindled. Even the American relief organizations began to run out of rice. Not enough planes came in to bring more food. The Communists had surrounded the city and stood only three miles north of the airport, the only escape hatch left. They covered the landing strips with rockets and the planes with gunfire.

"Look at that bridge," someone said.

"You mean the broken pieces of a *has-been* bridge," Cathy laughed. She could bring a smile into the most dreary situation.

"The broken bridge is one of the reasons why the Cambodians have to retreat. The government isn't getting enough supplies to the troops because they now have to do it by boat or planes only, and the enemy shoots everything to pieces," our missionary driver said.

"How did it happen that the bridge blew up? Didn't they watch it carefully?" I asked.

"The Communists smuggled enough dynamite in a Red Cross van, brightly marked as such, to the middle of the bridge. They jumped from the vehicle and the thing blew up. It ripped the bridge into pieces. The Cambodians had let the vehicle through because it was marked as an International Red Cross vehicle," the driver said grimly.

"When will people ever learn that Communists believe that their desired end justifies *any* means to get there? They couldn't care less what and *whose* rules or contract they break. There are no such words as 'fair' or 'international rules' in Communist vocabulary," I said and felt helpless anger rise in me. All I needed to see were those refugee rafts that had just been unloading. This time they made it—the next time they might not—and these rafts carried only women, children, and old people, nothing and nobody else. According to the Geneva Convention, such transports were permitted to go unmolested, but the Reds sank them anyway.

I tried not to think that below the waters I looked at lay hundreds of women and children who had still been alive when I came to Cambodia yesterday. Now they were dead, buried mercifully by a sluggish, polluted, narrow, flat river. This little body of water was the last protection that Phnom Penh had against a tidal wave of terror, hate, and heartless cruelty from people who believed that they had been called to conquer the world. My heart screamed: God, are You going to let them win at a time like this? Will the Communists be permitted to stop the wildfire of the Gospel that has begun to sweep Cambodia? Burn, you fires of God, burn and spread fast!

17

We Are One in the Spirit

After we left the river we drove to the Cambodian headquarters of Jim's organization for a short morning worship service. The native relief workers gathered for special prayer and singing. Most of it was in their native language, but some prayed in English.

I shall never forget their national leader. They called him Vaughn. Short of stature like most Cambodians, he stood ever so tall in spirit when he prayed. He sounded like a child—trusting, simple, and so deeply dedicated to helping his people. He prayed for more food supplies, for wisdom to help the refugees better, for protection for his family while he was so busy and gone for days and nights. He asked God to bless the Americans for all the help they sent to his land. Finally he said, "Father-God, You know that we love our homeland, Cambodia. Please do not let the enemy erase this little land of ours from the map, let us be and stay a Cambodia that has freedom to pray to Thee."

His voice broke and the lump in my throat got so big I couldn't swallow or talk. The war noises boomed loudly into the stillness that followed his prayer.

"God," my heart said, "will Cambodia become another Lithuania or Estonia, that Communism swallowed and erased after World War II?"

We looked into the workshops. Little fishing boats were in the making, and high stacks of raw plywood lined the walls.

"What are those and what are they used for?" I asked.

"These are little crate boards that cased American explosives and ammunition sent to Cambodia by the United States. We save every little piece of wood to built houses for refugees," a native said.

I shook my head. What an irony! The outer shell provided shelter after it had brought a means of defense and death to this land. How typical of all that is human! There are always the light and the dark, the yin and the yang, the love and the hate, the good and the bad—and all so very close together!

Our next visit took us to a very special orphanage. Little did I know what the next few hours would hold for me. It looked like an ordinary Cambodian house structure, but it had a wire-mesh fence around the yard and it appeared and smelled very clean. Over the gate was a big sign: "Angel's Christian Orphanage." A smiling young Korean man in his late twenties welcomed us. He was the orphan director and the only "Father" of the place.

Before we saw the orphans, we visited with him for a while. He had a Korean name, but everybody called him Jimmy.

"How did you become an orphan director," I said to Jimmy, who looked much too young to be in a responsible position of any kind, "and how did you come from Korea to Cambodia?"

The young man bowed politely and invited us to sit down. A Cambodian servant brought tea, and we sipped it the Oriental way while Jimmy told us his story.

He became an "orphan" before the age of ten when the war tore him away from his family. His mother had no way of feeding her children, so Jimmy joined the streetboy groups in Seoul. The boys survived mainly by swimming out to the big ships and skimming the waters around them for floating grain that had been spilled and for other edibles. They'd gather it by the handful into a rusty container or in discarded aluminum cans. Then they would swim back and build a little fire in the street to dry themselves and cook the rice. They also polished shoes for a few coins.

"See this big scar under my chin?" Jimmy said, "I got kicked by a Korean whose shoes I didn't shine fast and well enough. It was in winter when it happened, and I nearly bled to death!"

Another time he swam out to a ship and got stuck in silt and seaweeds when the tide went out. He was trapped until after long hours the tide came back in and lifted him enough that he could free himself and swim back.

The rough street life taught Jimmy many skills needed for survival—

good things and bad things alike. One skill Jimmy learned very fast and soon became an expert in was karate. Another thing the boy picked up word by word was the English language. As he shined the shoes of American GIs they befriended him, and it wasn't long before Jimmy taught American soldiers karate and was paid well for it. Now he could help his mother a bit, but he didn't return to her home. His mother didn't fit into his rough philosophy of life anymore. She was a Christian, and she let him know that she prayed for him without ceasing.

"I had no place in my life for my mother's God," Jimmy said. "I wanted to succeed, see the world, go to America!"

When the Americans looked for people who could pass the civil service test, Jimmy dared to take the Korean-English test they required, and he passed. The American Army sent him to Vietnam to supervise an American aid program there. While in Vietnam, Jimmy met a high Cambodian officer who invited him to come to visit him and his family in Phnom Penh. It happened while he stayed with them that he noticed the streetboys and orphans of the capital linger around and beg as he once did.

He tried to ignore them. After all, nobody had worried about him. Nobody? Would he have survived if absolutely nobody had ever cared? Jimmy became friends with a few of the streetboys, and it seemed only natural that he would let them sleep on the floors of his little rented place. By the time he had collected ten of them, his landlord threw him and the boys out of the little apartment. Jimmy had some dollars saved, so he leased a little house. After his boys and he moved into the house, Jimmy had a dream one night. A white-robed, shiny figure stood before him and looked so very kindly but sadly into Jimmy's eyes. The man had a can of gasoline in his hand that he poured over Jimmy's clothing. Jimmy began to burn. The fires covered his entire body and Jimmy awoke, bathed in sweat and deeply frightened. The fire had been so real and hot in the dream that he could hardly believe that he wasn't truly burning when he awoke.

Jimmy understood the meaning of his dream well. The God of his mother was warning him. In every letter his mother pleaded with him to accept the Savior. In every letter she spoke of her prayers and about her fears that he would end up in the fires of hell. No, Jimmy didn't want to burn, but he didn't know exactly what else to do either. The next day he slipped into an empty church, and there he sat and cried before God. He did it for several days that way and made sure that nobody would see him there. After all, a big-muscled karate expert like Jimmy didn't want people to know that he was afraid and confused and cried like a little child before God.

God moved into Jimmy's heart and life when at last Jimmy invited Him in. He knew immediately what God wanted him to do. Jimmy went into the streets of Phnom Penh and collected the children nobody wanted. He, who really didn't like children at all, became an orphan father, and he filled his house to the brim with children.

When we visited the place, he had ninety-six orphans in his place from the age of six to fourteen. Several Cambodians worked with him to take care of all of them. The diet was simple: big pots of rice, some vegetables, meat when available or given to them.

"How do you pay for everything, Jimmy?" I asked.

"My brother in-law is in the United States and sends me through the Korean church in Los Angeles $100 a month," Jimmy said.

"You can't feed ninety-six children on $100 a month," I said.

"I know," he said humbly, "but some American friends who were GIs here sometimes send me money, and American organizations help me when they have rice or medicines left over. And whenever we are in need we have an all-night prayer meeting!"

He got up and took us into the classroom. Every child was in uniform. The boys wore white shirts and navy blue shorts, the girls white blouses and navy blue skirts. All had socks and tennis shoes.

When we entered, the kids rose respectfully and in silence. Jimmy smiled and gave a signal, and ninety-six Cambodian children burst into singing.

"We are one in the Spirit" they sang in English, and their clean-scrubbed faces smiled and shone with the great appreciation of our visit. Nothing could have hit me more. Tears streamed down my face, and I had no way of stopping myself. Orphans are hard on my emotions at any time, but those faces got to me like no other group ever had. Was it because they looked so vulnerable in their trust toward us, or was it because war thundered to the north of us while they sang so innocently at the top of their lungs?

Jimmy gave a little speech in the native language, Bill whistled for them, and Cathy sang while I walked among the little desks and looked over shoulders into open books and lesson studies. I also studied the wall charts. Everything in that place centered around the Bible. The children were divided into many groups named after Bible characters, and Paul's group competed with John's group and Sarah's group for stars in performance, cleanliness, and highest grades.

I smiled under my tears. Jimmy obviously ran a very tight ship—he had to—and I wondered how much individual attention the kids received! Some had typical orphan symptoms, I noticed. Several little boys sucked their thumbs fiercely, and a few little brown hands reached after me when they thought I wasn't looking. Orphans have a great need to touch someone. I knew something about that urge as a child myself!

They clapped after every performance and sang some more songs for us; then we waved to each other because they had to get back to their classwork and we had to leave. As we walked out of the room Jimmy said, "Last night we had another all-night prayer meeting." I stopped in my tracks and looked back into the little, brown faces that were still gazing after us with big, dark, now sad eyes.

"Oh, Jimmy," I said horrified, "how could you? Why didn't you let them sleep today, how can six-year old children come to class after praying all night!"

"They must study," Jimmy said seriously. "They must keep up with their work!"

Jimmy carried great burdens. We all prayed together before we left the orphanage, and Jimmy prayed in his mother tongue. I didn't understand a word except the word *Jesus (Yay-zoos)*, but I watched tears stream down his face as he poured out his heart to God. He was only a big boy himself, I thought, with bulging muscles and tough karate skills. He carried a big scar not only under his chin but in his soul. He had grown up under the shadow of rejection, and he knew little of normal family love and tenderness, but he was so eager to do the best as he knew it.

I gave him a big hug before we climbed into the car and handed him my card. "Jimmy," I said slowly and deliberately and I meant every word of it, "from this moment on your orphans are *my* orphans, too—and you are *all* mine, okay? I always wanted an orphanage of my own; I found it today! As long as I have life and strength, you will have all the help that is needed. Write to me, let me know, and we in America will help you. Remember, you have now a new older sister: Hansi. We are tied closer together than by family blood; we are related by the blood of Jesus Christ!"

Jimmy looked at me. It took him a few moments to understand what I had said. When it sank in, a big smile covered his open, boyish face. "Thank you, my new sister, Hansi," he said, "thank you. I will write to you. I will forever remember what you said—and will pray for you!"

The car pulled out and I wiped my nose and eyes. I knew something had happened inside of me and I would never be the same again. Little brown faces had gotten into my heart, ninety-six of them. God had given me another desire of my heart—and with it a great, new responsibility.

18
The Wrath of Men Shall Praise Him

If I thought that the visit to Sut Thong in the Central Highlands of South Vietnam had left me with unforgettable, sober impressions, Cambodia's plights tore my heart so deeply I felt wounded and raw inside. How much suffering can a feeling person witness before one either grows numb or cracks emotionally? I felt myself come close to a cracking point and wasn't sure how much more I could handle. My crisis moment came when we visited the biggest hospital of the city—a civilian hospital that was filled with casualties of the war, soldiers and their families alike. The wards, hallways, and every bit of space were overcrowded with cots, people, and commotion. More wounded Cambodians streamed in incessantly.

The head doctor, a short stocky man, received us for a few moments. He spoke English with a French accent, and he acted most courteously toward us.

"Sir," I asked him while a wounded young mother and her bleeding little baby were carried in right past us, "how many doctors are at hand to take care of these many wounded and sick people in your hospital?"

"Madame," he said, "we have forty-three doctors. They are all in surgery right now, and I should be there myself. Our problem is not a lack of doctors but a shortage of medical supplies. We are desperately in need of sutures and other surgical aids that are needed to sew the people back together!"

I felt myself go tight inside. What an irony! When wounded people arrived at the hospital thinking that, at last, they had it "made," forty-three doctors couldn't help them very much because they'd run out of simple medical supplies.

I heard some excited talking and commotion in one corner of the ward, and I asked what was the matter. One refugee woman who had just come in, spoke rapidly and in a deeply agitated way to the group that surrounded her cot. She shed no tears but was obviously badly shaken.

"She watched another raft go down and approximately three hundred mothers and children drown in front of her eyes," someone translated to me. "The Reds told the fleeing families to come back after they had pushed away from the river bank and when they didn't obey, the Communists shot at them. One raft exploded and sank!"

That did it for me. I couldn't listen anymore, and I felt that something within me was ready to burst wide open. I couldn't cry in front of all those suffering people who acted so bravely, tearless and resigned to their fate. I walked away and stood on the wide steps in front of the entrance. Outside, under the blue sky and the glaring sun, I took some deep breaths. I felt sick to my stomach from the smell of dried blood, vomit, dust, urine, and many other hospital smells, and my heart screamed to God: "Why, Lord?" I cried inside and looked up. "Why do people have to kill each other because they believe the wrong thing? Why, when You, oh, God, did provide *the* answer in Your Son Jesus? Why must the Communists ravage this land so badly? These people here are gentle and sweet and so helpless."

"The wrath of men shall *praise* Me," God answered me as clearly and distinctly as if a person had spoken, and I stopped screaming inside. I tried to understand what had been said to me. Was it a Bible text? Most likely, although I couldn't recall it as something I had ever consciously been aware of, but *how* could that text be applied to what I had seen and heard the last few days? (For text *see* Psalms 76:10.)

"God," I whispered to myself, "how can these inhuman cruelties of war and Communism praise *You*, a God of love? How must Your perfect loving heart suffer when You see Cambodia so mangled and torn to pieces. God, what do You mean?"

It hit me like a flash, like lightning out of the sky. A new insight pushed my depression and misery aside, and God's omnipotent reassuring wisdom rose like a new dawn in my troubled soul. I heard Eugene's voice say again inside of me what he had said at the breakfast table: "The

Gospel of Jesus Christ is spreading like wildfire through Cambodia. Hansi, what we have been waiting for is finally happening."

And I could see and understand God's Word. This whole agony and "pain with a thousand teeth" made sense only in the light of eternity. God alone could turn such evil into good and bring beauty out of the ashes of a nation. It wasn't God's original plan for the Cambodians or for any of His beings to suffer and to go through so much woe and grief, but when the devil gets his way and by his scheme and design he tries to thwart God's plans, God turns around and brings about His will anyway. It *is* God's command that the Gospel of Christ shall be preached in all the world. And when people cannot grasp it in any other way, God even turns the evils of war into His saving power and brings out of it a great harvest of souls. Thousands of Cambodians had to experience anguish and pain as never before, but because of it many will be forever in God's kingdom. Some day they will praise God that they were permitted to "suffer for a little while" (See I Peter 5:10).

I nodded into the blue sky and felt my unshed tears burn away. "Forgive me, God," I prayed, "I should know by now that You never make a mistake. May Your will be done here in Cambodia and all around the world!"

From that moment on I could see and do what had to be seen and done until we left Cambodia, and God kept my heart in perfect peace.

We visited a refugee camp outside the city that consisted mainly of new converts to Christianity. They had pitched their shelters around a small church and worshipped together every day—in shifts. The courage of these people strengthened my just-found-again peace. Jim's organization had helped them to relocate when the enemy neared.

"When the Communists find out that certain families or villages have accepted Christianity, they kill the children in front of the parents to break the spirit of our new believers. The men are forced to join in the fighting, the women are taken as slaves into the rice fields," I was told.

Most of the people had saved nothing but a blanket, a mat to sit or sleep on, a pot to cook rice in, or only the few rags on their backs. They sat under big plastic sheets fastened to bamboo poles and smiled at us. Yes, they smiled and waved and the children crowded around us, some stark naked, some dressed only in one piece of odd clothing. A few chickens ran among the many feet and pecked at the dried weeds in the hot, red dust, and everybody seemed content to be alive. A few men were busily working. Each family had received a crude hoe and a sack that contained seeds to plant, some rice to eat, and a few other basic necessities to make life under a plastic sheet in the broiling sun of the Cambodian dry season more bearable. Not many men were available. The camp consisted mainly of women, children, and old people, but the few who could swing a hoe got ready for the monsoons.

Never had Cambodia waited as desperately for the rainy season as when we were there. Rains would not only bring another rice crop but the interruption of the fighting, a few months when people could live, heal, and breathe! The rainy season would widen the river and make the riverbanks swampy and the pathways unpassable. The Reds always had to stop the offensive when it began to rain. Everybody waited, looked, and prayed for the rains, but the monsoon was still several weeks away. Would the defenses hold up until then?

Jim never once saw his friend, the government official, while we were in Phnom Penh. The man had not left the defense headquarters for many days, we were told. That Cambodian had sent his three children to America during a previous offensive, and Jim was eager to see and speak with the father to assure him that American families were looking after his children. I had met the two younger ones and could have verified it—an American Christian doctor and his wife kept and treated them like their own children.

After a second, restless night Friday dawned and not too soon. Everybody felt physically and emotionally drained and exhausted. Ann was sicker than when we came, and I couldn't wait to get her back to a place where she could find the medical care she needed.

Missionaries, Bible translators, relief workers—they all came to tell us good-bye. The living room of the mission guest house was filled with people. The atmosphere seemed ominous and oppressive—everybody tried to put up a good front but a big question hung over all of us. Would our plane be able to take off and get out? Would the rest of the people who stayed behind be able to get out in case of a Communist takeover? Nobody talked about it, but everyone knew the odds.

I looked at Cathy. "Hey, how about singing, Cathy? Why don't you sing 'our' song before we have to part?"

Cathy nodded. She reached for the recorder and pushed the button for the accompaniment and then her beautiful voice rang out once again.

Because He lives, I can face tomorrow,
Because He lives, all fear is gone . . . .

Tears came and were wiped away, smiles appeared, and the air in the room became light and easy to breathe. God took the healing power of music to comfort, reassure, and bring renewed peace into troubled hearts. Nothing is too hard or too threatening for His children—just because He lives! The last high note filled the mission guest house with the sound of triumph, and in that spirit we piled into the car to go to the airport.

Ann looked weak and pale but smiled her usual sweet smile. I remembered to pour boiled water from the refrigerator into my little unbreakable thermos bottle that I carried with me everywhere because I knew that safe drinking water was simply not available in the Orient. An hour later, at the airport, I thanked God that I had that water in my purse. Ann had gotten up to take some pictures of a plane that was just landing, and refugees and exhausted soldiers poured out of it. Suddenly she handed me her camera with the heavy lens and said, "Hold it, I might drop the thing."

I grabbed for the camera and then for Ann. She was fainting. The place was too crowded for her to have fallen, and many hands reached out to help as soon as people became aware of her illness. We got her to sit down, and people moved so that she could lean against the wall. I poured her some water and she revived.

"God," I prayed, "help us to get out of here soon. Ann needs a bed and a doctor fast!"

A stewardess showed up out of nowhere and said kindly, "Follow me!" I helped Ann up, and we were told to get into the plane before the other passengers crowded in. We climbed in and found a place where she could stretch out a bit and get some fresh air.

Not until the plane was ready to take off did I realize that God had done another miracle for us. The small aircraft was so full of people, luggage, smoke, and noise that Ann would have had no chance in her weak condition even to get into the plane. The people who boarded after us pushed, struggled, argued, and fought, for too many had tickets and had waited for too many long hours to get on the plane.

The pilot took off the way he had landed, straight up and away!

Stories had it that the Communists were only one or two miles from the airport—whatever, we got out without being shot at!

Ann sat at the window and I could peek out sitting next to her. I shall never forget my last glimpses of Cambodia. Burning boats and constant explosions below us laid a gray veil over the dark green jungle and the yellowish muddy river that twisted around the totally surrounded city. Phnom Penh was completely closed in by the enemy. The airport was the last escape hatch to the outside world. How much longer would the runways be open?

19
We *Want* to Go!

I never felt more relieved about a landing than when the wheels touched the bumpy ground in Bangkok. Ann needed a bed and so did the rest of us, but it took several hours before we got our heart's desire. Customs dragged and nobody was at the airport to receive us. So we stood around and waited while Jim tried to make some phone calls.

Ann sat on a suitcase and I stayed close by. The rest of the group wandered about, which wasn't easy because the place was so crowded that it took skill to get anywhere. People and congestion were not the only hazard, we found out; the uneven cement floor had unexpected surprises, too. I heard some noise and commotion, and when I left Ann to see what had happened, I found our Doris sprawled on the ground. When she got up, she couldn't use her right foot, and the ankle began to swell immediately.

By the time the mission vehicle arrived a weary group piled in. Doris hobbled on one foot, supported by her husband, who didn't look too well himself. Ann tried not to faint again. The mission guest house had not received Jim's letter, but enough beds were found to get us all settled.

"You are lucky we had room for you," Sandy, the housemother, said. "It is also not as hot as usual at this time of the year, so you should have a good night's rest!"

After a light supper we all found our beds. Doris was in bad pain, Ann too sick to eat, and Jim and I talked about the days ahead. The itinerary showed a three-day visit in Thailand, and then we would fly to Bangladesh.

"Daddy Jim," I said, "I am not so sure that Bangladesh is in God's plan for us. We'd better pray about it!"

We did, and it seemed that God was closing every door into Bangladesh. The flight there was cancelled, we couldn't make contact with the Bangladesh mission guest house, not by telegram, phone, or letter, and the rumors about the present situation there didn't sound good at all. The hotels charged $30 or more per person a night, food was scarce, and typhoid was on the rampage. Of course we had been vaccinated, but we all were either sick or low in resistance and too tired to put up a good fight against any epidemic disease. Maybe God wanted us to stay longer in Thailand? It surely seemed that way.

Olin took his wife, Doris, to an American mission hospital the next day, and they found a broken bone. She came back with a heavy cast on her leg and hobbled in on two crutches. Ann was obviously fighting malaria attacks. She began to freeze and chatter one night so badly that her teeth and bed shook. Several of the group struggled with dysentery, but I didn't. I took my charcoal tablets faithfully. Although some people smile about me because I trust simple home remedies so much, I believe in it! I know what charcoal and herbs can do for me. I never travel without it! It has saved my health many a time. I swallowed my black tablets cheerfully twice a day and was ready for action. What do You want me to do, Lord? I wondered. Plenty, I found out, a lot more than I had anticipated.

First I spoke in the International Church on Sunday night. I had a hard time doing it; I still felt too upset about Cambodia. Word had gotten around by Sunday morning that Phnom Penh might not last through the weekend. The Communists were advancing steadily, and the airport was being torn up by rockets.

We all prayed and cried together on Sunday morning, and every Christian church in Bangkok had special prayer services for the safety of their missionaries, none of whom had come out.

I was torn with worry not only for all those missionaries we had left behind. I couldn't keep from crying every time I thought of "my" orphans and Jimmy, the young orphan director. I told Ann on our flight out what I had found in that Angel's Christian Orphanage, and her first question was, "Did you leave any money for food?"

I looked at her aghast. What was the matter with my head? I forgot to give my Korean Jimmy some money. In every other orphanage we had left a gift; why would I forget to do it in a place where the need was greatest? I talked to Roger, one of the leaders of Jim's organization in Thailand about it, scolding and chiding myself for my unexplainable thoughtlessness.

The man looked at me. "How would you have given them the money?" he asked in his Australian accent.

"By traveler's check," I said. "That's the only kind of money we carry!"

"Then it is good that you forgot," he said. "The only money that buys food in Cambodia at the moment is their own currency, and the banks will accept only international checks. If you give me your checks, I'll exchange it into valid Cambodian currency, and we will hand-carry it in to Jimmy, I promise!"

"You mean it was perhaps of God that I forgot to leave money in the orphanage when I did?" I asked, very relieved.

"It surely was God's direction," Roger smiled. "Your help wouldn't have done Jimmy's orphans any good, but the way it will be done now, they can buy rice immediately!"

I handed him as much as I could spare and still make it home somehow. We had no idea what expenses to expect in Africa, but I knew that God would see us through, even with very little money left.

"How do you hand-carry the money in?" I asked Roger.

"Sharon and Peter are flying in Monday morning, and you will meet them tonight at a dinner!" he said.

We had dinner after the Sunday night service in one of Bangkok's leading hotels. They served American-style food. What a treat! Sharon and Peter did a strange thing. Whenever the sugar was passed, they took a cube and slipped it into their pocket.

"How come you are putting sugar in your pocket instead of in your coffee?" I asked Sharon.

Sharon had the young, innocent face of a little girl, but she was in her early twenties I was told. She was also one of the nurses in the Nutrition Center for starving babies we had seen while in Phnom Penh. She was spending a few days in Bangkok to rest up.

"Oh," she said and blushed a little, "there is no sugar available in Cambodia, and we are taking those few cubes in as a special treat for the staff and kids alike."

"You can have my sugar, too," I laughed. "I don't use sugar at all and I will give you my share!"

The rest of our group decided to give their sugar, too, and the pockets of the two young missionaries soon began to bulge. The native waiters watched us closely, and the whole deal was funny enough that we laughed and joked about it. We Americans obviously puzzled people around us, but the funniest thing happened when we ordered dessert. I always asked for papaya, pineapple, or some other native fruit in season, but some of the group decided to splurge since the menu offered ice cream and other Western specialties.

Roger was undecided. "Try one of the American ice creams," I said. "I know they have a butterscotch dessert that is delicious—someone recommended it to me."

Roger ordered butterscotch, and the waiter looked terribly puzzled. When he returned, he brought two things: a dish of ice cream and a glass of scotch.

"Roger," I said, "I didn't know you drank alcohol for dessert." I grinned at him. He looked bewildered and then blushed. The whole thing struck all of us as hilariously funny, and we all laughed except him. He acted deeply embarrassed.

"Take that stuff away," he said to the waiter. "I didn't order *that!*"

The waiter looked at him in amazement. Why would anyone refuse a glass of good scotch? He took the dessert silently away, but his face spoke volumes.

"Oh, those crazy Americans!" he seemed to think. "Who could ever figure such people out? First they pocket all the sugar, and then they send back, untouched, a perfectly delicious dessert."

We laughed and teased Roger a lot that evening, but beneath our light conversation and chuckles sat a deep and consistent worry.

"Sharon," I said when we finally got ready to part, "isn't it dangerous for you both to fly back into Phnom Penh tomorrow? The rumors we heard today don't sound too good!"

"I know," Sharon said. "We got in touch with the Center by wireless radio today. We were told not to come back in because things are so uncertain, but we will try to fly in anyway. They need us too much. We are still understaffed even if we make it back!"

"What is Peter doing?" I asked. Sharon, a nurse from the Midwest of the United States answered for him.

"Peter is from Australia," she said. "He is setting up an X-ray machine for us. It will help to diagnose TB and other problems in our babies so much better."

"I have got to go back in and get it done fast," Peter said with a big smile. "My wife is expecting her first baby in March, and I promised her I'd be back in time for the event!"

I looked at both of them. They looked young enough to be one of my own children, and I wondered how I would feel if my own son or daughter were to fly back into Cambodia against orders! Sharon looked so painfully young and vulnerable, and young bearded Peter would be a father soon. What if anything happened to them?

Missionaries are a special breed, in any country, I found out more and more.

Sandy and Tom, who took care of the mission guest house we stayed in, on the edge of Bangkok, were another special couple.

Their older children went to boarding school, one little girl was below school age and still home, and Sandy expected another baby. The new baby was due within a few weeks.

"What will you do after the baby arrives?" I asked the young mother of three, since I knew they were planning to leave Bangkok.

"We are planning to go and help in Cambodia; they need more missionaries urgently," Sandy said with a big smile.

"You mean, you will take your newborn baby and your little girl and go with your husband into Cambodia? Have you been there before and do you know the extent of the war and problems at hand?"

"Oh, yes," she said, "we visited Phnom Penh just a few months ago. I know what I am getting into—but you see we came to the mission field to lead people to Christ. How could we pass up such a great opportunity to spread the Gospel? I am praying that my baby will come soon. I know I wouldn't have enough medical aid to deliver over there or we'd go right now!"

I swallowed hard and didn't know what to say. Living twenty years in American affluence had made me a bit soft, I figured. Everything in me opposed the thought that anyone would voluntarily take a newborn baby into the midst of war, germs, and danger, but Sandy obviously had not one question in her mind about it. She couldn't wait to go—and she smiled!

Thailand is a land of Buddhism, and Christianity has had a hard time making inroads into it so far, I found out next. The only native people I got acquainted with were Christians and didn't necessarily reflect the thinking and habits of the common people.

"Thai people are fighters," one Christian retired U.S. Army officer told me. He should know. He had married a Thai girl much younger than himself, and they were expecting their first baby.

"She has accepted Christianity," he continued, speaking of his young wife, "but she fights at the drop of a hat and so does everyone else in her family. Thai people are by nature fierce, suspicious, and often radical, especially when young!"

The young people do have great influence in Thailand and are the ones mostly responsible for the anti-American spirit that could be felt at various times, I was told.

"The students are very radical and most likely Communist infiltrated," one missionary said. "They stage their coups and get their way. They got the prime minister toppled, and they are determined to get the Americans out of Thailand. It's nothing but a matter of time before the United States troops have to leave, and most likely it will be the end of American Christian missions, too!"

When I visited one of Bangkok's famous Buddhist temples, the place thronged with people, all of them deeply absorbed in one thing: to worship Buddha. I had wondered why so many orchids and flower chains were sold everywhere. Flowers overflowed at little stands, and youngsters peddled them at every street crossing when the lights turned red. I had wondered if the Thai people were such great flower lovers because even the poorest seemed to purchase flowers here and there.

Our visit to Thai temples gave me the answer. The flowers were laid on and hung around every statue of Buddha. Some of the statues seemed buried under thousands of orchids and other flower chains. The odor of wilting flowers mixed with the strong scent of heavy incense and the human smells gave me a feeling of oppression, but nothing pressed as deeply on my soul as the expression of despair I saw on the many faces of those who had come to worship. I watched one woman kneel before one of the statues, completely unaware of my watching her. She was too absorbed in her act of worship. She bowed and prayed with moving, silent lips numerous times, and then she would throw her two little plastic oracle pieces. Nearly everyone carried these pieces, made of wood, plastic, or hard glass. With them, Buddhists receive the answer. If the pieces fall just right, it's a "yes"; if they fall in an awkward way, it's Buddha's "no."

That little Thai woman agonized, pleaded, and threw her plastic pieces again and again. It was obvious that the Buddha didn't like her that day, and fate was against her. She received a "no" every time, and her gestures turned more and more frantic. I stood and watched and my heart ached. She obviously believed with all her heart, and all she received from it was more agony, more hopelessness, more despair.

I wanted to talk to her. I wanted to tell her that belief isn't enough, even sincere belief in something that had been passed on to her by her ancestors. One had to believe in Truth to find the right answers for life and death. The God of the Universe has provided that Truth and the answer for *every* human being in His Son Jesus, but most of the people on this earth don't know about it yet. They haven't even so far heard the name of Him who can save and heal and bring peace.

I wanted to share my hope with her, but I couldn't. I did not speak her language and even if I did, I couldn't have spoken to her about my Lord in that temple. I might have ended up in a Thai jail, something a foreigner tries to avoid at any cost.

"The Thai people have a very simple system for law, order, and their traffic," one missionary lady had explained to me just a day before. "Whenever it concerns a foreigner, especially an American and a woman on top of it, we are wrong. In an accident we pay regardless who is at fault. The Thai people love to take a Westerner to jail, and they demand unbelievable bail prices to let one out."

What problems, injustices, and difficulties our missionaries so often have to face! Amidst opposition, unfairness, and ingrown prejudices, they try to show people in darkness a better way of life. How discouraging it can often be!

"Yes," another missionary said to me and he looked a bit grim, "once in a while I get very tired of the way we are treated here. We came to Thailand to help but most of the Thai people don't want our help, only our money—and they try to get it by hook or crook—mostly the latter. They'll cheat us whenever they can—they fine us whenever possible. If someone claims that the 'Ugly American' is out here oppressing and exploiting the natives, let me tell you something: He is only defending himself!"

"I think it is especially hard for Americans amidst foreigners to accept such a dishonest, unfair value system," I said, "because it is hard for any American to understand the Oriental mind. Americans have a very basic, strong sense of fairness and justice. It's a result of the Christian ethics that have prevailed for the last 200 years in our land. Orientals have a completely different sense of ethics and values. They believe in the survival of the fittest. I have been told that they go and offer Buddha a special gift of thanks after they have managed to cheat on someone and gain by it!"

"You are right, Hansi," the man said thoughtfully. "It is often hard to understand why people can be so corrupt and selfish without feeling guilty about it, but they simply don't know better!"

"That's why God sent you here," I smiled into his sober face, "so that they may know and learn what God has to offer."

He smiled wistfully, "All we can do is sow seeds. God will have to grow a harvest in His own good time. The Gospel *is* spreading in the last years much more rapidly than ever before, but we are not reaching the masses. Only a small percentage of the Thai people turn to Christ. Strangely enough, the North shows the greatest increase in Christian converts at the present time. It's where Thailand has the heaviest infiltration of Communism that the people also open their hearts to the Gospel of Jesus Christ. The South has also had great hardships lately because of devastating floods. Whenever missions go in to help those who have no home or food, the people reach out for more love!"

I thought of Cambodia, but I didn't say anything. I just wondered: Would it take a Communist attack to open Thailand for the Gospel of Christ?

20
Doctor Puppy and God's Promises

The moment the word spread among the missionaries in Thailand that our group would stay longer than planned, invitations to speak flooded in from many places. I didn't mind it. I needed to stay busy to keep my mind off the grave situation in Cambodia, but I was greatly concerned about Ann.

She felt too weak even to get up. She was confined to bed and four, white-washed walls of a small, simple room with only a cracked, old ceiling to stare at, and the unbelievable racket that came in with the foul smell through the open screens of the windows was hard on her.

The mission campus was surrounded by poverty-stricken Thai huts on stilts that were stuck in swampy grounds and polluted standing waters. Every imaginable filth rotted in those still, slimy waters. Mosquitos swarmed everywhere, and I wondered if the Thai people tried to keep these blood suckers out of their open huts by noise. Nobody was so poor, it seemed, that he didn't have some kind of a noise machine, be it a transistor radio or an old record player cranked by hand or whatever. Each neighbor tried to outdo the other. One hut next to Ann's room managed to drown out the rest, and it was American hard rock and roll that did the trick!

Poor Ann! She tried hard to be brave when all the rest of us would leave every morning. Even Doris had learned to get around on her crutches, and she kept up with all the sightseeing.

"God," I prayed, "isn't there anything that could brighten Ann's days a little bit?"

She couldn't even read her Bible as much as she wanted to, her head hurt too much. What could we find to make her days a bit more colorful?

God is never so busy that He cannot take care of even such small requests. I found what I was looking for when I walked into Tom and Sandy's apartment one morning. Their older son held the sweetest little puppy in his hands. The little dog's face and eyes seemed covered with golden-brown bangs; the whole creature was one wooly, wiggly, tiny bundle of charm and cuteness.

"Where did you find this precious little dog?" I asked and took the puppy into my arms.

"We brought him from Cambodia. We couldn't help but fall in love with him, and knowing that dogs don't have a chance to grow up and live there because people steal and eat dogs, we just couldn't bear the thought and brought him with us to Thailand. He has a bit of a better chance here," Sandy sighed.

I handed the warm little cuddlebug back to the children.

"Would you do me a favor?" I asked. "Would you go to the room where the sick little lady is and take that puppy to her? She loves puppy dogs more than anything else in the world, and it would make her day if she saw this doggie!"

I had to rush out and leave, but the doggie was taken to Ann that day (and the days after). I could tell when I returned home that evening because Ann had a new spark in her eyes.

"The doctor was here," she announced, "and I feel much better!"

"What doctor?" I said because a nurse had looked after her and given her medicines so far.

"Doctor Puppy," Ann smiled. "He crawled all over me in 'leaks' and bounds, and I had so much fun watching him!"

Ann will be forever convinced that besides God it was Doctor Puppy that made her well. As she began to get up and go downstairs to visit her little friend, she found out that she had a harder time seeing her new four-legged friend. Every time she got near the doggie, Sandy's little daughter would grab the dog and run. She permitted anyone of us to hold her pet but Ann. That smart little girl had it all figured out: Ann would take the doggie with her when she left and she wasn't willing to let her playmate go, so she had to watch out for Ann. It brought much laughter to all of us, and everybody was intrigued with Doctor Puppy and the little girl's grave concerns. I thanked God that Ann was recovering. We had wondered if she would have to interrupt the trip and fly back home.

The week in Bangkok did all of us a lot of good physically and spiritually. God not only used me as well as others of our group to strengthen the missionaries and their families; he used missionaries to encourage me and fill my spiritual needs.

One of the richest blessings I received came out of a prayer meeting I attended one morning. English-speaking Christians of various denominations and different walks of life who lived in Bangkok had begun to meet together for sharing and praying. It would have been impossible just a few years before to attempt such a thing because the various denominations had been so hostile to each other. Missionaries of one denomination wouldn't even so much as speak to each other or greet each other on the street, I was told. One was afraid the other would snatch their new converts away if they became too familiar. Things looked up and a new spirit of love and brotherhood had begun to fill some people. Out of it came informal prayer meetings and new Bible study groups.

I attended one of the study groups. We sat together in a big circle and everyone sang, listened, shared, and prayed. I looked at the earnest open face of an American missionary called Paul who was in the group and tried to follow his words. I had a hard time because I couldn't shake my deep burden about Cambodia. The reports had gotten graver every day. He was saying:

"America to me means missions. She *is* the leading nation in sending the message of Jesus Christ to the world. That is her great hope and why she is so blessed. If her mission spirit ever ceases, the strength and vitality of America will also cease. The many Christians in America are the salt of America. America is the salt of the nations. My future as a missionary and minister ties into the future of America. I wish I could know what it will be, but all I know is that God as a loving Father has everything under His control. We are called to be His body, and we express God's will and emotion to the world. Since we are His flesh and bones we have God's promise that not *one* of His bones will be broken."

How could he say that the bones of Christ's body were not broken? He looked straight at me. "God is impressing me to share a text with you: Psalms 105:19."

I opened my Bible and read it: "Until the time that his word came: the word of the Lord tried him."

I felt more puzzled yet. What did this text have to do with my worries and concerns?

Paul went on: "God gives His church and children promises. He gave promises in Old Testament times to Joseph, to Abraham, to many— God gives promises to us today. God's promises are trials in our life until they are fulfilled. Remember Joseph: He received his promise in dreams, dreams that upset his brothers and even his father. In order to have his dreams come true, Joseph had to go through many trials, but he maintained the right attitude and God fulfilled His promise. He always does because God bases His promises on Himself, not on our circumstances. When we think of Abraham, he had a promise, too. Until it came true, it was a sore trial to him, so much so that he tried to help God out— and so did David. We all do that. We often wonder if we can trick God into His promises. We cannot do that, for circumstances never enter God's promises.

"If we Christians would only remember that God always keeps His promise regardless of how hard it is to wait for God's time, we wouldn't be so burdened or judgmental in our thinking.

"I, myself, have to remind myself often that God has given me a promise for my ministry. Sometimes it looks so discouraging. The young people here are so set on taking drugs and following all the modern wickedness that one can but wonder how God will finish His work here in the Orient. But we need not worry: God *will* do what He promised and circumstances will not stop Him. When God gives you a promise," Paul said and looked straight at me again, "you have to believe and wait!"

I knew God was giving me a message to comfort my burdened soul, and I felt more at ease. Somehow I couldn't grasp the full meaning of what was said, but I was sure that some day I would fully understand. All I knew was that God had given me promises for my personal life and ministry as He had for Paul. As for Cambodia and my orphans, I carried God's Word in my heart about that problem, too. I needed to keep my mind on God's promises, not on the disheartening circumstances—that was God's message for me!

21
Booms and Hunger

The days flew by; we knew that our stay in the Orient would soon be over. We were scheduled to leave for Beirut as a stopover, and the following day we'd fly into Africa.

We had spent more time in Bangkok than anywhere else so far. I couldn't help but wonder why. I knew I'd leave many friends behind, Christians and non-Christians alike because God had opened so many opportunities for me to speak in various places. Why would God use me so much in Thailand when in other previous countries I had to turn down so many invitations? And *why* did we not get into Bangladesh, a land that was so much in the world news? I got the answer to both questions in God's own time—and I found out that God's timing is *always* perfect.

The mystery of the closed door into Bangladesh was solved for me at a dinner engagement. I almost didn't accept the gracious invitation; I had been too much on the go and felt too tired to smile anymore. I get what I call "peopled out." That disease catches me every time I go from meeting to meeting and dinner invitation to church potlucks without rest and time to meditate. However, I accepted because the American hostess was disarmingly sweet and kind, and she mentioned that someone who worked in Bangladesh would be at the dinner, too.

His name was Jim, and when I met him and his family, I understood why God had not let us go on into Bangladesh the week before. Jim and his wife managed the only mission guest house in Dacca but were spending their Christmas vacation with friends in Bangkok. If we had gone to Bangladesh, we would have been stranded—and that with Ann as seriously ill as she was and Doris with her leg in a cast.

If anyone was an expert on Bangladesh, I found out, it was that Jim. He and his family had been sent there in 1958, long before the revolution came. When war broke out in 1971, they decided to stay. Only two foreign families lived during the entire nine months of fighting in Bangladesh. Jim and his family suffered many hardships. They lived at that time in the little town of Feni, then in East Pakistan. Eleven days after the revolution broke out, their four children were caught at a play area near their house by the attack of two jet fighters of the Pakistan air force. Cherrie, at that time thirteen years old, sent her sister to warn their parents while she held her two little brothers down to the ground. The planes made their first attack right over their heads. The children got away unharmed.

Cherrie wrote a poem about that frightful experience just six months later, while the war was still roaring. The children had learned to stay close to the house and crawl under furniture whenever military forces of West Pakistan attacked. They saw grief, hunger, and death and Cherrie wrote about it. The father handed me the poem with his girl's permission. When I met her, she'd grown into a pretty teenager of seventeen who attended a mission school in India with her sister Kathy. Their vacation was almost over, and they would go back to school soon. Cherrie's poem ripped old memories open for me. So much of it I would have said the same when I was her age—except for the last line!

> Roaring out of the Bengal sunset they came,
> Two black dots on a warm summer evening.
> Some children stop their playing to set clear eyes
>   upon them,
> In awe watching the pair, soaring over rice fields
>   and straw huts
> Like finches looking for some place to rest their
>   wings.
> But suddenly as they spot the tiny town,
> Their nature changes, and now, like vultures,
> They screech and dip down upon it.
> A piercing wail rings out and then,
>   BOOM . . . BOOM . . . BOOM

The children scatter like frightened ants into their
houses,
Amid the constant shattering and blasts.
Flinging themselves upon the floor,
They lay frozen in fear.
Their faces ghastly, their blood cold, their heads
buzzing with the question, "Why?"
While outside, the vultures peck at their prize.
A mother tries to comfort a child with shaking hands.
The only steady comforting sound is the thunk, thunk,
thunk of the father's feet
Pacing the floor.
Again and again the planes dip
and again and again
BOOM . . . BOOM . . . BOOM
Then in the same mysterious way they appeared,
They are gone.
All is quiet. The world seems dead.
But . . . off in the distance comes the clattering of
wheels on the old road,
And the jingling of bells.
Like water from a broken dam,
The living gush into the countryside,
Trying to escape from the smell of death and blood.
Some crying, some with faces of stone,
They all plod along together.
Not saying a word,
Not having to, because their grief is written on
their faces.
Slowly, they all filter away.
The night comes, the stars twinkle,
A cool breeze blows from the south.
The only irritating sound is the crickets
which seem to say,
LOVE YOUR ENEMIES . . . LOVE YOUR ENEMIES . . .
LOVE YOUR ENEMIES.

I learned some facts about Bangladesh during that dinner that I
hadn't known before. Bangladesh is the eighth most populated country

in the world, small in size but filled with 84 million people, most of them hungry and many starving.

"Why, Jim," I said, "why is the need so great?"

"The war brought destruction of land and crops, and the recent floods have destroyed thousands of acres of crops. So the families gather up their few belongings and trek to the next town or city. Thousands of poverty-stricken families continue to stream into the capital. All they find is more misery, hurt, and hunger. Bangladesh is by far one of the poorest lands on earth."

"How do Christian missions relate and how *much* is done for these poor masses?" I asked.

"Most people are Moslems. Dacca was once a proud center of Islamic culture. Now it is flooded with beggars, people who live on sidewalks and on the outskirts of the city in shantytowns and hunger camps. Only a half of one per cent of the population claims Christianity; the rest follows the Moslem faith. Many Western organizations have come in to help, but let's face it: regardless of what can and will be done, before the next harvest up to three million people will have died of malnutrition!" Jim said quietly.

The food in my mouth became hard to swallow, and I blinked tears.

"Isn't there anything *more* we could do, *anything?*" I asked.

"We have to help one person at a time and leave the rest to God," Jim said kindly but matter of factly. "You see, the Islamic philosophy of life compounds the problem at hand. People resign themselves to fate without too much struggle. It's Allah's will! So they lie down and die. The government is trying desperately to bring some order into the chaos. They send field kitchens into the refugee camp to feed the hungry people some gruel every day. Some people perhaps ate too fast or were too far gone and died after eating. So the stories spread that the government had put poison into the food to get rid of the poor. Now the government has to force the people by gunpoint to eat. They are afraid to touch what *is* available!"

When I left after dinner I was so deeply shaken that I understood *why* God had not let me go into Bangladesh at that particular time. God has promised that He will never put more upon us than we can bear. That promise covers everything in His children, even our emotional tolerance level.

I knew I couldn't have handled Bangladesh right after Cambodia. I was still raw inside from the suffering I had had to observe there. I wouldn't have been able to watch those naked swollen bodies with the thin, shiny, scaly legs lying in doorways, on sidewalks, and in open fields waiting to die. There is a silence that comes with starvation, I was told, an eerie silence when people still shed tears but they can't make noises anymore, they are too weak for it.

Little children have no strength left to resist the simplest forms of disease. They are not claimed by cholera, dysentery, typhoid, or typhus; they die of colds or measles. Their little bodies shrivel up, left alone because the parents have died already, uncared for, with flies covering the body. Thousands of children must die—and it won't be their fault!

I wept myself to sleep that night and tried to figure out why I belonged to the elite of this world who are permitted to eat three meals a day or more if they feel like it. I had no answer. I could only thank God for my privileges and promise Him to do all in my power to help wherever possible. I knew I wasn't better than my suffering Moslem brother. I was only better off for I knew of a hope that reached into eternity. And on top of that I had the privilege to be an American and live on this earth in peace and plenty. I would never understand all the whys, but I knew one thing: I'd never be the same again after this world tour! I could never again take all my blessings for granted, and I could never again keep all my affluence to myself. I might not be able to help the millions, but I surely could help one or a few at a time.

I wasn't the only one who felt that way. Our entire group became closer knit in a new compassion for a needy world. We knew that we would go back home to the United States and spread the word. If the Americans could only *see* what we had seen, they would be willing to help. I knew for sure that Americans as a majority believe in helping, and one happening on our flight to Beirut assured me anew in my convictions.

22
One at a Time

Tom had driven us at midnight to the airport outside the city of Bangkok. Our plane was to leave at 2:00 A.M. While waiting to board the plane, I saw a blond Western woman in her mid-twenties with a handwoven basket in her lap sitting quietly and obviously waiting for the plane as we were. Something attracted me to the scene, and I worked my way to her side. When I got a glimpse into her basket, I saw the tiniest, cutest, brown-skinned baby face I had ever seen.

Before I could strike up a conversation, the loudspeaker announced that passengers were to board the plane. I was relieved to see that it was an American airline. The last few flights had been Oriental services, and the cramped seats and other inconveniences had been hard on some of us weary travelers.

I watched the woman and basket vanish into the first class area and was disappointed—I wanted to talk to her so very much. I just knew that I would find an interesting story, but would they let me sit in the first class long enough for an interview? They did! The plane was almost empty anyway, and the stewardesses spent a lot of their time around that basket, too. They almost acted as though they owned the woman and that little doll. Jane, the girl with the basket, was an employee of that airline, I found out. She was most gracious and very eager to tell me all about her *new* baby from Bangladesh. No, she wasn't adopting it for herself; she had no time for that. Furthermore, she was single and would have a hard time getting permission to keep the baby in the United States. The future parents of the child waited in New York, hoping and praying that she would arrive with a baby. She almost didn't!

"It is so hard to untangle all the red tape," Jane laughed. "If you think the United States is bureaucratic, try the Orient!"

"Aren't the Bangladesh people glad when you come in to help and save lives?" I asked.

"Most people are—they stick their necks out to help. People *are* wonderful," Jane said warmly. "Of course, some natives will spit at me because I walk the streets as a woman without a veil and in a short Western skirt, and beggars will fall all over me. It is hard to see the starving children who chew betel nut to kill their gnawing hunger and watch begging mothers jab their children to make them cry as a Westerner approaches just to obtain my sympathy and maybe a coin!"

As for the red tape, she knew many tricks by now.

"In order to fight your cause, you get yourself briefed on the immigrant rules of that specific country, know the ground rules well, and use one rule to fight another," Jane said with a wistful, tired little smile. She looked rather weary, and her eyes appeared bloodshot.

"Yes, I am very tired," she admitted. "I have had only two hours of sleep within the last thirty hours. I have been on the go for the last nine days to get this little girl away!"

"Do you work for an adoption agency?" I asked her.

"Yes, as a volunteer," she said. "I make my living as a counter employee of this American airline in New York. I can fly free to any place this airline goes on the whole globe. I use my spare time to go to various countries to get orphaned babies out. Of course, I pay a bit of my own to sit in first class, but it gives me more room for the child. Sometimes I have to take extra days off without pay to accomplish a mission.

"This trip is typical. I will have missed ten days by the time I get back, and it will take me several weeks to make up my lost time. It's a miracle that I am bringing her with me; it looked hopeless at first. Everything seemed to be against us. I found her in a Catholic nuns' orphanage. They find newborn babies so often at the door where starving mothers put them during the night. This little thing looked as though she could endure the long trip and make it. Sure, she carried fungus and signs of malnutrition, but it cleared up with proper food and treatment after a few days."

"Did you have what was needed for her?" I asked.

"I surely did, and for a few others, too. I carried 120 kilogram overweight luggage into Bangladesh with me. The hassle wasn't with the American airline but with the native line into Dacca. I did what I do with all the other officials of a foreign country. I walk in and act like I assume that they will surely help me. So they do!"

She laughed heartily.

"I carried milk powder, medication, and baby food—all given to me in America," she said. "People are *wonderful!*" She sighed.

"My greatest problem was that offices in Islam countries close on certain days. I knew I had to get back by Wednesday, and the only official who could sign the permission had gone to Delhi. So I got on a flight to track him down and found out he was in a big hotel attending a dinner in his honor. I had no place to stay in Delhi, no native money and no transportation to the hotel. An American lady who found out on the plane what I was trying to do offered me a place to stay, and her nephew drove me to the hotel. I sent the official my card and told him I needed to see him on urgent business. He came away from his meal and signed the paper between courses. I flew back and got the baby ready. The native airline demanded a passport and a bank clearance for the baby. I took the passport picture with my Polaroid camera, argued and got her passport into my hand within three hours. I got everything else, too, including £200 sterling against my personal check and a taxi to the airport!"

She turned her eyes up and gave another deep sigh. "The taxi broke down. When I finally arrived at the airport, the flight was full and closed. I marched into the manager's office. He promised me a seat if someone didn't show up. Thirty-three sailors *didn't* show up and I got my seat!"

I looked at the woman and the sleeping child. Jane had given her a bottle, and the little thing was a picture of contentment and peace.

"How much longer before you arrive in New York?" I asked the tired woman.

"If we have no more delays in Beirut, we should make it within the next thirty-two hours," Jane said.

"No more delays," I laughed. "Have you ever left any Oriental or near-East airport without delays?"

We'd left Bangkok at 4:30 A.M. instead of 2:00 A.M. as scheduled and felt very lucky.

"I hope I get in on time," Jane said. "I have already lost so many extra days. My airline is very understanding toward those of us who are involved in this rescue work, but I don't want to push my luck!"

"Are *more* girls involved in such work?" I asked surprised.

"Sure," Jane said quietly, "it was a girl named Pat who started it. She brought orphans from Vietnam. People have the idea that we airline people lie on beaches all over the world in our spare time, but many of us are involved and help each other like a family. We just don't talk too much about it!"

I nodded. Americans in general don't talk about the good they try to do at home or abroad; only the Ugly American is described in books and news.

"Tell me, Jane," I said, "are you a Christian?"

Her open face turned toward me. "I am not a churchgoer, if that is what you mean," she said quietly. "I wouldn't have time. I often work thirteen or more days straight through to accumulate free days for a trip. I believe in God and love. I read once a statement by Albert Schweitzer in the *Reader's Digest* that sums up my philosophy. It goes something like this: 'I have always held firmly to the thought that each one of us can do a little to bring some portion of misery to an end.' " Jane's face shone radiant in spite of her fatigue.

"Look, I can't help the millions," she continued. "Organizations try that and have their hands full. The small organizations don't have enough supplies. The big outfits are often not reliable or organized well enough. There are incredible problems with distribution of food and transportation. Food waits, freezes, and rots while people die. Natives are inefficient and corrupt and channel the stuff on their black market. So it can get very disgusting and it often seems so senseless for us Americans who try to help. As for me, I know what I will do. I spread the word and let it be known what individuals *can* do. I have many on my team!

"One of my friends lets her children sacrifice desserts, ice cream, and extra treats. The pennies for them go into a piggy bank. The money buys food for hungry children when I fly into the Orient. Those children feel that they have a part in my rescue work.

"I also sell handicrafts I bring out with me. This baby basket is handmade, and I'll sell it as soon as the baby is delivered. Americans will pay good prices for it to help me with my expenses.

"I might not be able to save them by the millions, but I can snatch *one* life at a time. I battled for ten days for this child. If I had not gotten her out now, she would have died of diarrhea before I could have gone back to get her!"

The baby opened her eyes, lifted her thin arms, and yawned. Then she closed her dark eyes again. Jane had slumped over the basket ready to fall asleep while sitting up. I helped to fasten the basket beside her with a seatbelt into an empty seat and watched her stretch out for a little nap. I knew she wouldn't dare to fall asleep deeply. Her ears would stay tuned in to the baby's cry for the next thirty hours or whenever the plane finally landed in New York. There she would hand this tiny brown bundle of life to the rejoicing couple who had waited for her a long time. Then this single young woman would go back to work the very next day!

A Bible text came to me as I got up quietly to return to my seat in the tourist section. I had read it in my small New Testament just the day before: "The Christian who is pure and without fault, from God the Father's point of view, is the one who takes care of orphans and widows, and who remains true to the Lord" (James 1:27 LB).

I fastened my seatbelt and watched the stars grow dim. A new day was born and I prayed. I thanked God for the little life that was spared, and I thanked Him for people like Jane.

Bless them all, God, bless and keep them in the spirit of Your love, even though they have no time to go to church and profess religion.

I can snatch *one* life at a time, Jane had said, *one* life, that's all— and it is enough in God's eyes.

Yes, it is all anybody can do, I thought—one at a time. If everyone who could would try to save *one*, millions would live—not only for now but for eternity.

Bless you, precious Jane! If you were my daughter, I'd be so proud of you!

23
Seventy Dollars or No Go!

I knew that we would have a short stop over in Teheran. The Arabian countryside before we landed looked strangely picturesque to me. It was rugged, naked, brown. It was bare desert without much vegetation, but there were countless human dwellings in various and unusual designs and forms. The entire panorama was dominated by the many high, smoke-spewing stacks of the oil refineries. The air seemed saturated with smoke, and the city reminded me of Los Angeles on a *very* smoggy day. We seemed to dive into a dirty, grayish-brown blanket when we finally landed.

Several people boarded the plane, and a young girl sat down beside me. She looked like an American to me and she was. Her parents were in the oil business in Teheran, and she had spent Christmas vacation with them. Now she was on her way back to the States to continue her college education. We chatted like old friends.

"Tell me," I asked her, "I didn't know that Teheran had smog. Is it always as bad as it looks now?"

We had taken off and the heavy layer of poison looked so thick, I wondered if people could see the sun. The girl nodded soberly. "Yes, and sometimes it is worse. It is one of the greatest problems Teheran has, being surpassed only by the problems of congested ground traffic on the many narrow streets!"

"You mean, Los Angeles and other American big cities are not the only ones who struggle with smog and traffic problems?" I laughed.

"Listen," the girl said, "give me American cities any day! At least they try to find a solution. Teheran just accepts it, it seems. People don't worry too much about what they breathe or when they arrive as long as the money comes in!"

"Is there an anti-American spirit among the Arabs toward your parents or you or Westerners in general?" I asked.

She looked surprised. "Oh, no," she said and shook her head. "Everybody is tied together in one common interest: oil!"

I nodded and looked down at the vanishing city and the barren deserts below. How strange that most of the earth's black gold would be below the most desolate dry ground of the globe. The pulse of the great nations was determined by the uninterrupted flow of that crude oil, and many people worked in heat and smog to bring it about. These people worked together in harmony, the girl said, and she added, "And why shouldn't they?"

"Yes, why not?" I replied and thought about the many times when the oil issue nearly had started another war among the superpowers within the last few years. I also knew my Bible well enough to look down there and realize that I looked on land that some day in the future would echo under the feet of many armies who had come for battle.

Armageddon is not dismissed any more as a fantastic scare prophecy of some simple-minded religious fanatics! Armageddon is a present, threatening possibility that nonreligious scientists and socialists predict and warn about.

I had heard about the Middle East and Bible prophecy from childhood on. This was the first time I had caught glimpses of it. I felt elated and disappointed at the same time. This mixture of feelings continued after we landed in Beirut, checked into the hotel, and went for a walk. To think that I walked where the cedars of Lebanon grew, trees the great King Solomon spoke about! I wanted to believe that the trees looked much taller and statelier when Solomon walked under them; the ones I saw looked rather stunted to me. I couldn't believe that that could be *all* there was to the Lebanon of the Bible. Buildings looked run down, the streets were littered—was the Middle East just an extension of the Orient?

I talked to Ann about it. She had seen the Biblelands before and enjoyed it. She felt disappointed, too. It wasn't the same city she had seen before, she said. Things were deteriorating, and one could sense hate and tension in the air. Daddy Jim gave us strict orders not to go out into the streets by ourselves and to inform him at all times where we were going, even as a group.

Our hotel looked out over the bay, and the white-capped, emerald-green waters of the Mediterranean Sea under the evening sky lived up to my expectations. It was breathtaking!

I didn't feel like going places; I had a severe sore throat and a very upset stomach again. So we retired early. The hotel met Western standards, and I had the first hot shower I had had in more than a week. The mission guest house in Bangkok had cold showers most of the time! I took another handful of my charcoal and crawled under clean, cool sheets.

We took off the next morning for Lagos on the East Coast of Africa. We flew with an Arabian airline, and the aircraft seemed loaded to the bursting point. The seats were designed for shorter, smaller people, and most of us sat very cramped. We sat and waited two hours while they tried to find a mechanical problem. At last we got off the ground, but the many hours of flight dragged endlessly, and I felt sicker as time went on. When we finally landed, Jim gave very clear orders.

"Don't let *anyone* carry your luggage," he shouted. "Let's stay close together. Follow me!"

That was easier said than done, we found out when we finally poured out of the aircraft into the terminal. The airport was so crowded, one could hardly move. Several young African men pounced on us as we struggled with the luggage.

"Porter needed," they shouted. We surely did, but I knew better than to nod. If Jim said not to do something, we'd better obey! He had been in Africa before and had had some hair-raising experiences that he told us about after we finally left the airport.

"The last time I was here," Jim said, "I made the mistake of letting one of these cutthroats carry my suitcase. He carried it from the gate to the front of the building and demanded fifty dollars for it. Luckily, the missionary arrived just in time and he argued with the porter. I finally got off by paying five dollars!"

The black fellows caught on fast that we wouldn't let go of our luggage. So they looked for other victims and ignored us. They did more than that! They cut in front of us and kept pushing us back in line for the custom clearance. We ended up as the very *last* to go through customs. By then I felt dizzy and sick and had just one desire: a cup of

tea and a bed. Never did it look more hopeless than that Sunday afternoon in Lagos, Nigeria, that I ever would get into a bed again!

Nobody was there to receive us, and Jim went to make some phone
calls. None of the numbers he called answered. He had the address of
a mission guest house and decided to get us there by taxi. He went to
bargain with some taxi drivers and found out there was no bargaining.

We had been watched closely by those fellows, and they must have
guessed our predicament. One tall bully of a fellow was the spokesman
and spoke enough English to answer. Jim showed him the address and
pointed to us eight people and twenty-one pieces of luggage.

"Seventy dollars," the man said lazily, "and we go!"

I watched Jim's ears turn red and knew what it meant. Jim could get
fiercely angry if someone played him dirty, but Jim kept his cool. He
knew better than to show his anger. The air felt heavy with hostility.
He tried again to reason with them.

Some dirty grins: "Seventy dollars or no go!"

Jim came back to us. He looked upset.

"I am not going to give in to them if we sit here for the whole night,"
he said. "Just for the principle of it, I will not let them get away with
it!"

Ann looked up. "All I know is that Hansi is sick and has to get into
a bed," she said quietly.

I sat on my suitcase and leaned against a pillar. I had the feeling the
airport was turning around and around. Faces of people came into focus
and vanished again, while heat waves and chills ran up and down my
spine.

The airline had handed us anti-malaria pills with the last meal, and
I had taken all I dared to take before we landed. I was a sick girl and
I knew it. "Jim," I said, "couldn't Cathy talk to those fellows. Maybe
they'd treat her better since she is black, too!"

"Never mind the color," Jim said grimly. "It's not our white faces,
it's the fact that we are Americans that they treat us that rotten! Cathy
is as American as we are, and they couldn't care less that she is black!"

Jim was so right. Several hours later, when he finally had reached a
missionary and the man drove up to get us out of our predicament, we
rejoiced. The missionary took us to a private home for supper, and at

last we arrived at the mission guest house late that night.

Comfort, the black housemother, looked surprised. "We were told you wouldn't come," she said in utter amazement, "and we had no reason not to believe it. How did you ever get your entry permission? Nigeria gives no visas to Americans; they are not too welcome in this land."

I couldn't worry too much about international hard feelings between America and Nigeria at that point; I was ready to faint.

Comfort had no anti-American feelings, it seemed; she was warm, concerned, and quick. She saw to it that I got into a bed—lumpy and old as it was—that had mosquito nets without holes over it. The windows also had pretty good screens. They didn't keep all the mosquitos out, however, and Ann spent half of her night chasing mosquitos that managed to get under our nets.

I didn't sleep too much, anyway. I tossed with fever and body aches, and my throat burned like fire. What a place to get sick, I thought.

The next morning found me drained and very weak. Jim called from downtown with more disturbing news. The group had been scheduled to fly into Niger by Wednesday. I was sure I'd recover by that time. Jim let us know that the airline that had scheduled us didn't exist any more. So we had no reservations at all! A tiny chance existed, however, to get on another airline as a stand-by that *very* afternoon.

Ann looked alarmed. "You are in no condition to fly out this afternoon," she said. "We just have to stay behind until you are well, and then I will get you out of Africa as fast as I can!"

Jim didn't like Ann's idea, but there was no alternative. He hated to leave us two women behind. I encouraged him to go on without us. All of us had looked forward to seeing certain parts of West Africa, mainly the bush hospital where Jim's son-in-law worked as a missionary doctor together with Mary Lou, one of Jim's six children. Jim had hoped to meet with influential officials in Niger and work out the details for the digging of a well for the hospital.

Jim came into the room and had prayer with us. He looked troubled. Then everybody packed in a hurry and left, already late, for the airport.

When he left, it suddenly hit me. We two women were not only in an inconvenient situation; we found ourselves unexpectedly in a very grave position: Two white American women, alone in a land where people hated Americans, with no reservations to fly out, both not well, and both soon to be broke because we hadn't anticipated the high prices in Nigeria. Even one week's stay would more than deplete our money.

I sat up in bed and watched the station wagon pull out. For one moment I felt real deep panic grip me. Then I thought of God and relaxed. "God," I prayed, "I have no idea why we had to come here at all. Whatever Your plans are, we can trust You. I thank You for looking after us and getting us safely out of here. Make us a blessing to someone before we leave!"

Ann reached for her purse. "I'm going downtown right now to see about flight reservations to get you out of here!"

We had prayer together and I handed her my passport and ticket. If anything happened to her, I'd be stuck in the middle of Africa without anything, I thought.

She smiled at me. "Don't you worry about a thing," she said. "I'll put up a good fight. You pray and I'll find us a flight out—either into Switzerland or Rome. God has never let us down, He'll come through again for us!"

I couldn't help but laugh. Ann had that resolute glimmer in her steel-blue eyes. Whenever she looked that way, the world had better watch out! It was for that certain big Dutch determination in her little frame that people in America called her "Hansi's little general." I watched her walk out the door, and I was pretty sure that Ann would find a way. She would at least give it a good try.

I lay back under the mosquito net and waited.

24
Crocodile Soup and a Hairdo

The late afternoon hours dragged, and the sun dropped past my window screens to the west. I watched a lizard crawl up the inside wall of my hot, sticky room. These lizards were everywhere and looked so ugly it turned my stomach. Some of them were bigger than my two hands laid against each other. They had the camouflage color of the African red, dry earth, a yellowish dirty-brown design on the back, and the bugging eyes stared without blinking.

Comfort came into the room with a cup of soup. It had a brownish color like the lizard on the wall, but it tasted good. I hadn't eaten for quite a while.

"Comfort," I said to the friendly black woman who spoke fluent English, "I do not know what kind of soup this is; it tastes good but in case you cook these crocodiles to make it," I pointed at the lizards, "don't tell me. I don't like your African crocodiles; they turn my stomach!"

Comfort held her stomach, she laughed so hard. Tears rolled down her cheeks. She laughed while she found a broom and chased the one lizard out of my room, and I heard her laugh in the kitchen while she told the kitchen boy about my crocodile soup. She never got over it, and we laughed and joked about it every time we saw each other. It was the only thing I laughed about that afternoon; the rest of the time I prayed and worried about Ann, who was out there somewhere.

It always amazes me how fast the night falls in the tropics. All of a sudden it was dark again, and Ann hadn't come back. The bell had rung for the evening meal. I went to the dining room. We had finished when the door opened and Ann marched in, a triumphant look on her face.

"I got confirmed reservations for a flight to Switzerland on Wednesday," she said and dropped into a chair.

Comfort saw to it that Ann got some leftovers for supper, and then we went to our room. Just as we walked out of the dining room the telephone rang. It was the missionary who had taken Jim and the group to the airport. He asked Ann how things were going.

"Fine, thank you," Ann said, "we have reservations to fly out the day after tomorrow."

"You mean you got the request for two reservations," the missionary said indulgently.

"No, I have the confirmed reservations with SwissAir to fly out from Lagos to Geneva on Wednesday," Ann said patiently and had a twinkle in her eyes.

"Are you sure?" the missionary said. "This isn't the United States; this is Africa and people don't get reservations within a few short days. It often takes weeks to get out of Lagos!"

"Maybe so," Ann said in her no-nonsense tone of voice, "but we are leaving on Wednesday!"

We did, and how it came about was one of God's special miracles mixed with Ann's determination. She told me the details while she tucked me under the mosquito net.

Comfort had called a taxi for Ann to get her to the office of the airline we had been booked with. Because we were not flying into Niger but straight out into Europe, the ticket had to be changed and signed off by several African airlines to a European airline. Ann had patiently gone from one office to another to get the necessary signatures. Returning to the office that had started her on this chase, she found the native official suddenly not willing to cooperate at all.

Ann tried patiently to explain that we needed to go either into Rome or Switzerland. The official questioned it. "Why don't you fly into France?" he said.

"We don't need to go into France. It's a detour for the rest of our trip into Central Europe," she replied and tried to keep her cool.

"But I think you should go via France," the black man insisted. "After all, if the other lady is sick, why would you want to run all over Europe?"

That did it for Ann. This man had sent her running all over the city for the entire afternoon, promising that he would arrange reservations when she returned. Now he stalled.

"Look _____!" she snapped at him while rising to full height. "We don't want to go to France, and we are *not* going there!"

She looked at the employee at the desk next to the bully who hassled her and said, "Can you call SwissAir for me and find out if they have any flights open within the next few days?"

The other man was obviously enjoying the fight and the fact that the little bit of a white woman dared to stand up against that big fat boss of his. He obediently dialed as told and reported back almost immediately:

"Yes, two seats are free on Wednesday morning into Geneva."

"Book it," she ordered, "and tell them I am coming to their office immediately!"

She turned to the man who had tried to ship her to France and said, "Now release the tickets to SwissAir."

He looked at her and tried again, "Maybe I *can* get you on stand-by to Rome."

"Forget it," Ann said coolly, "please release us to SwissAir *now.*"

He took his time, Ann told me, for he knew that it was almost 5:00 P.M. when all offices closed. He wanted Ann to miss the reservation to Geneva for some reason.

Finally, he handed her the stamped tickets, and she shot out the door and ran down the street to the SwissAir office. People everywhere were locking up their shops. Ann knew that by now it looked hopeless to get into any office.

"I prayed and ran," Ann said, "and when I got to SwissAir the door was still open. I rushed in and one man was still in there, talking on the phone. He was a native, very friendly and efficient. He verified our reservations and shook his head when I told him all the hassle I had had during the afternoon."

I chuckled to myself as I pictured Ann with that bully.

"Ann," I said, "I have *never* heard you swear before. Are you sure you said what you said?"

"I surely did," she said resolutely, "and I'd say it again under the same circumstances. That fellow was obnoxious and I knew why. He wanted me to pay him a bribe, and I was equally determined not to pay him off. Furthermore, we are too broke to pay anything but our bills!"

"What made you so late coming back?" I asked next.

"The taxi," she said grimly. "That's another wild story, my dear! I walked out and showed one taxi driver the address of the mission house. He quoted an outrageous price. I knew what I had paid coming in when Comfort had arranged it, and I gave him exactly that offer. He just sneered, so I walked away and approached the next taxi driver. Suddenly the first guy came after me and tapped me on the shoulder.

"What do you mean, going to that driver? I gave you a bargain!" he shouted.

"No, you didn't," Ann answered. "I gave you my offer—you either take it or leave it!"

"Get in," he frowned.

"At *my* price?" Ann asked.

"Yes," he replied.

"He got even with me anyway," Ann laughed as she continued her story. "He took one of his buddies home, and it was a long detour. When we finally got downtown, the traffic was nearly at a standstill. Every street was full of vehicles, and the noise and dust were almost unbearable. While we waited at a bottleneck, he turned to me and growled. 'You see this traffic? I got to have more money to take you home!'

"I looked him straight in the eye and didn't blink once. 'I am in such traffic every day in Los Angeles,' I said. 'That's nothing special or new to me! We agreed on a price. Now let's move it!'"

He grumbled something and moved, and Ann got safely back to the mission guest house. She even paid him an extra tip after he had delivered her to the door, and he looked very surprised.

"It's just a matter of principle," she grinned. "These people think they can push me around because I'm not very tall. Well, I have news for them!"

It was easy to laugh about it after it was all over, but we knew that it was the protective hand of God which had done it all. We thanked God with joy that night and used the next day for rest and repacking. I needed more than that. My broken, dull mirror showed a rather wilted me. My hair hung limp and sweaty.

"Comfort," I asked more in fun, "is there such a thing as a beauty salon in Lagos?"

"Oh, yes," she said seriously, "one is right around the corner. Do you wish an appointment?"

I gave a sigh of relief and nodded. To think that I could improve my messy appearance before going into Europe eased my mind immensely. Comfort kept her promise and negotiated the appointment.

"It will cost you ten dollars in American money for a shampoo and set," she said. "The lady will call you when they are ready for you."

I winced when she quoted the price, but I was desperate enough to pay it. After all, everything in Lagos was outrageously expensive, even for the natives. Comfort paid the equivalent of one American dollar for one pound of sugar. She kept everything in the kitchen under lock and key. She couldn't afford to have anything stolen by the servants, and her eyes always looked pained when the guests used too much of anything, especially sugar or spices.

I had never paid ten dollars for a hairdo in my life, and I expected something special for such a price. I got it!

It took the operator half a day to get ready for me. I sat around in Comfort's guest room and read, yawned, and visited until I was called. The *salon* consisted of a small room overstuffed with aged magazines, old and new bottles, a broken sink, and one lone hairdryer. A girl brought in a rusty pail half filled with warm water. She had warmed it over the kitchen stove. No wonder it took so long to get ready! The shampoo and washing went quickly, however; the woman in charge had no intention of wasting too much water. After all, what if another customer showed up?

"Well," I thought, "as long as she gets it wet for the curlers, who cares?"

When she finally had found enough curlers in various boxes and drawers to begin the work, she seemed genuinely disturbed. "If I had known that you have so much straight hair, I would have charged you *more* than ten dollars," she muttered. "This hair is impossible to work with!"

I swallowed in silence. More than ten dollars? My hair *not* manageable? I was stunned. I ended up overwhelmed when she had me ready for the dryer. She had managed to put a few curlers on top of my head, with hair sticking out everywhere—and the sides bunched up on two huge pin curls each. My hopes of a sophisticated look for Europe vanished. Dejected, I hunched under the dryer when Ann walked in. She gave me one look and bit her lips; then she tripped over the cord and the dryer stopped blowing.

"God," I prayed and felt desperate, "not *that* on top of it. I need wet hair in this African red dust like crocodiles in my bed or in the soup!"

Ann managed to keep a straight face, and I ignored her deliberately. The dryer got fixed. My hair was half dried when the woman dragged me back to her chair. She pulled the curlers and pins out, combed my hair in a few determined strokes and looked triumphantly into the mirror.

"You like it?" she said with pride. I swallowed hard. I have a very tough time lying, even socially, but I knew better than to incense an African woman with the approximate weight of three hundred pounds.

I gave a weak smile. "It's very . . . unusual," I stuttered and reached for my wallet. I handed her ten dollars and a tip, and she took it with a lofty gesture. After all, it had been a bargain given by her to me and out of the goodness of her big, generous heart.

Ann pointed to her camera. Her photographer's heart was bleeding, I knew. She had not been able to take even one picture since our arrival in Lagos. Comfort's husband had warned us not to take pictures anywhere. The Nigerian people felt very defensive toward Americans who took pictures. Some Westerners had misused their photos to downgrade the Africans, and the resulting mood toward clicking cameras was ugly. It could end in smashed cameras and confiscated films.

Ann had no desire to take a chance. She had saved for years to get her good camera equipment, so she restrained herself. Would we leave Africa without any pictures at all?

I looked at the big African hairdresser in her bright muumuu-type dress and the unusual hairdo she wore. (I saw not one American "Afro" among the Africans; most women had their hair braided into many thin, long tight braids, bent and fastened at the hair roots.) "Ma'am," I said politely, "I would like to show my American friends a picture of an African hairdresser. Would you give me the honor of posing with me?"

She grunted an unwilling consent, and we arranged ourselves before her shop. Ann clicked fast in case the woman changed her mind. She did, and the second pose already showed a big frown. We grabbed our stuff, said a polite thank you, and hurried off.

We suddenly remembered another important appointment. Supper would be served shortly in the mission house, and we couldn't miss that! The meager meals didn't last too long anyway, and our stomachs growled from one meal to the next.

That evening while we packed to leave the next morning, Ann looked at me. "I think I have a great idea to get rich fast!" I gave her a suspicious look.

"Honest," she said and blinked her blue eyes ever so innocently, "let's start a little beauty salon in California or even in Europe. I am sure that other people would be delighted to invest with us as soon as they see your new hairdo. We could fly the African beauty-maker out."

I gave her one long grim look, and then we laughed a lot. It didn't improve my hairdo, but it made me feel much better. Humor puts things into the right perspective. So what if I looked like a scarecrow? We were leaving Nigeria in the morning—and I couldn't wait!

25
I'll Go Back If I *Have* To!

To get our flight reservations in such short time was a miracle. Little did we know that it would take a few more interventions by God to get us to the airport and out of Lagos.

The morning began very simply. We had breakfast and said a warm goodbye to Florence, who had been an American missionary to Nigeria for several years. She had come to Lagos for thyroid treatment. Since the doctors were striking in the hospital of her choice, she wasn't sure what would happen. "We have learned to wait," she smiled patiently. "Things don't move very fast in Africa."

We gave her some of our Western luxuries we had carried in our suitcases up to that point. Toilet articles, a book, instant coffee—things she couldn't get in her remote mission station. She seemed so pleased.

After we had paid our bill and recovered from the shock of it, Comfort called a taxi. When it finally arrived, I eyed it with concern. The vehicle was tiny—the smallest model of the Toyota. I wondered how we would get all our luggage into it. We ended by squeezing two more passengers and their luggage on top of us. One was a German missionary who had a street ministry in London and was on holiday in Africa. The other was a teenage boy who was on his way back to his mission boarding school after Christmas vacation. The two men folded themselves on the front seat. Not until the car moved did both of them confess their problems.

"I have no money," the German said. "The banks are on strike, and I couldn't exchange a thing." (It was a half truth!)

"I have to be at the airport in forty-five minutes," the mission student said, "and it's my only plane for today." (That was all truth.)

"Don't worry about the money," I said to the taxi driver, "we'll pay it. But can you make it to the airport on time to get this boy on his plane?"

The driver flashed his big white teeth. "I try," he grinned, "I do best!" He shifted back into second gear and laid his hand on the horn. Then he pulled from the street, which was jammed with vehicles, onto the nonpaved street shoulder. People, hand-pulled carts, bicycles, chickens, everything splattered aside as our tooting car raced along the dirt, leaving a big cloud of red dust behind. The path was treacherous. The earth had big cracks and deep holes in it from the extreme dryness of the season, and the little car seemed to jump like a grasshopper from hole to hole. It didn't hurt any of us too much. We were too tightly squeezed in and our laps were covered with so much luggage that we just bounced with the car. I only wondered how long even a car from Japan could take such abuse before an axle would break.

I couldn't help but laugh. The car's horn blared, the driver sweat profusely, and the German's face was a study in depth. He was obviously scared, and I felt rather amused. He seemed to be the type who manipulated people for free favors whenever possible. Such people irk me, especially if they claim to be Christians. Well, the man paid for this ride, for he had the scare of his life. He finally turned around when he heard me laugh out loud again and said sourly: "My sister, do you know what will happen if the police stop our taxi?"

I shook my head and smiled some more. Not until we arrived at the airport did I find out that any ticket given to the driver would have been charged to *us,* since the German had no money. Neither did we have very much, but God was with us!

After forty-six minutes we arrived safely at the airport. Since *every* plane leaves late, we knew the boy would make it. Ann paid the taxi driver with an extra tip since he had tried so hard, and our German passenger vanished without too many words of thanks. The airport seemed twice as jammed with people as when we arrived. We soon found out why.

Alitalia was on strike. Passengers had been stranded for the last two days at the airport and were trying to find a stand-by flight on other airlines. The line to the SwissAir counter seemed endless. We stood and stood and waited. Time ticked by. What if we couldn't get checked in before departure time? We prayed and waited. Inch by inch we moved toward the counter. The closer we got to it, the harder it became to move forward. The "porters" were pulling their old tricks again, trying to cut in and shove us back. We piled our luggage in such a way that they couldn't get close to us. Ann and I seemed to be the only two women in an endless line of men who fought their way to the counter. We obviously looked the most vulnerable and the best target for cutting in. We were pushed and elbowed from every side. Ann stood like a rock. She squeezed and wiggled and ended up at the counter. A big black man looked over her shoulder at the tickets she held ready.

"You better go first and pay your airport taxes," he growled at her.

Ann looked past him as if she hadn't heard. If she went to pay the tax, we would lose our place in line. She tried to hand our tickets to the man behind the counter; the man behind her reached over her shoulder and shoved a stack of tickets on top of our tickets. The employee of SwissAir looked up.

"She was here before you," he said firmly and shoved the man's stuff aside. He took our tickets. We put our luggage on the scale and he labeled it and then gave us our boarding passes. We had it made! At least we thought so!

We paid our airport tax and went to the boarding area. We stood for another hour and squeezed in among the first to be searched. Then we had to go through customs.

"Where is your money declaration?" a black man snapped.

Ann pulled it out of her pocket. It tore as she reached for it.

"What are you trying to do—destroy government property?" the man had an ugly frown on his face. He didn't wait for an answer. "How much Nigerian money do you have with you?" he demanded.

"None," Ann said politely, "we gave our last money to the taxi driver and for airport taxes."

Angrily the fellow waved us on. I had no question in my mind that he would have fined us for the torn paper if we had had any more Nigerian currency with us. Our luggage stood ready to be inspected by another big Nigerian. He made no attempt to open it. He just held his hand out.

"Mercy," I murmured to Ann, "we have no money left to pay him off. What if he gets nasty and pulls everything out of our suitcases. We are already late for the plane."

Ann and I searched through every pocket. We *did* find a handful of native coins and laid them into the open hand. The hand closed over it; the other hand marked a big X on our stuff, and the inspection was over. We walked out onto the airfield.

I'll never forget the sight. Amidst the red dust, the lizards, the litter and the dirt, the heaps of cement sacks and other various cargo stood a silver-white plane with a big cross on its tail. It looked like a shimmery bird of another world, and its door stood wide open.

We climbed the stairs, and a pleasant Swiss stewardess welcomed us aboard. We were led to the no-smoking section, and I floated dizzily into the air-conditioned, spotless clean comfort of a cushioned seat. Ann took my shoes off and covered me with a blanket. I was exhausted, drained, washed out—and too elated for words. I didn't even care that the plane did not take off for another two hours.

The pilot apologized several times in French, English, and German over the loudspeaker for the delay. "Our passengers are detained in the customs department; we cannot leave them behind," the man's voice said.

"Please don't," I thought, "nobody should be forced to stay behind. After all the hassle one has to go through to get to the plane, everyone should have a chance to leave this miserable place."

Passengers, who climbed in one by one, weary and upset, told about the harassment and erratic behavior of the customs officials. If the officials felt like it, they would just take a break and let the long line of people wait. Nobody could do anything about it. The people had to bear it without protest. Nobody *dared* to protest. Who cared if the planes stacked up on the runways?

We finally rolled out, and everybody gave a deep sigh of relief. The stewardesses in a short time had a delicious hot European meal ready and served, and it was time to relax.

Below us stretched northern Africa. I wondered about the rest of our group. Had they gotten safely into Niger? Were they treated as roughly as we had been? Did Daddy Jim meet with certain government officials to get permission to dig a well? I knew that the survival of his son-in-law's mission hospital depended on more water. The place was deep in the drought belt. For several years they hadn't had any rain in that part of the world, and the situation was getting more desperate every day.

It was not until we returned to the United States that I heard about the adventures and the safe return of our fellow travelers. I thanked God that we hadn't been able to go along with them. So did Jim.

"As much as I wanted you to see it all," he said, when we met weeks later, "we would have been in serious trouble if the group had been any larger."

Jim and the other five friends had left us for the Lagos airport. They had struggled as much and more than we did to get on a plane, since it was an African airline. They finally boarded and got called out of their seats twice.

"Why was that?" I asked Jim. He shrugged his shoulders.

"Did you have to pay a bribe?" I asked.

"I think they expected one but we had none to give," Jim smiled.

They got on at the very last moment. The officials either realized that these Americans wouldn't oil their palms or nobody else showed up to fill the plane. So Jim and the others got to fly north. Part of the travel to the mission hospital on an old truck was far from easy. It was dust, heat, thirst, and human misery all the way.

Death stalked the African desert. The earth was cracked so wide open that animals and children could have fallen into the dried crust of the ground. Not a blade of grass had grown for years. The cattle were gone —and the people had died by the hundreds and thousands. The hospital needed water. Food and drink were unbearably expensive.

On their flight out, Jim's party had to sit for a whole night in a tiny, miserable airport. They boarded a plane in the early morning hours and were dumped at the last moment. In spite of reservations and Jim's protest, they had to get off the plane and watch the aircraft take off without them.

"As furious as I was," Jim said to me, "I found out later that God makes *no* mistakes. The very next morning I met a high official who okayed our well project. I had tried and tried before to make headway, but every door seemed closed. God waited until it looked hopeless to open a way, so that we might know that it is His power that regulates the affairs of His children." Jim and I nodded.

"We eventually got out," he smiled, "and we all lost some weight in the process. One cup of coffee and a piece of toast cost nearly five dollars —believe me, we didn't eat too much! When we finally boarded a small plane to leave, I thanked God that we were only six. We had to sit on each other's laps as it was. My legs almost gave out in the process!"

We had a good laugh. It's easy to see the humor of a tough situation when it is all over. I pictured my six tired, hot, and bedraggled fellow Americans pushed around and treated rudely. It didn't change their attitude, however. They could laugh about it and were as eager as ever to help.

The comment Cathy made to me when we met again was typical of the Christian spirit: "I told God that I'd go anywhere He sends me, even back to Africa. Should it be His will to send me to Lagos, then I need a very clear and special order. I would even go back there, but only if I *have* to!"

I agreed with her. Of all the places in the world I would like to visit again, Lagos is not on my list. Nevertheless, American missionaries live there even today to preach the Gospel. They struggle with malaria, the anti-American spirit, a soaring cost of living, and an uncertain political future. They are there because God gave *them* a very clear and special order. Only God knows how much longer they can stay.

26
Why Are We in Geneva?

I had asked Comfort at our last breakfast why the Nigerians disliked America so much.

"I am not from Nigeria," she smiled, "and have no ax to grind with either side, but Biafra left a bitter taste in the mouth of these people."

"What do you mean? Wasn't it right for America to help the starving people during your civil war?"

The African housemother smiled again. "We listened to both sides on the radio at wartime and heard about the great suffering in Biafra. Actually, the Biafrans should have won, for they had the help, the war material, and the sympathy of the Western world. The people here in Nigeria believe that it was their prayers that turned the tide and kept Nigeria from being divided. There was no retaliation when the war finally ended. Our head of state is a sincere Christian, and he called both sides to restoration and brotherhood. I was at that time with a Christian medical team, and we entered Biafra right after the cease-fire. I couldn't believe how many well-fed, normal people we found in Biafra. As a matter of fact, the government called in an international commission to disprove all the bad propaganda about Biafra."

I nodded. I had read the speeches of Nigeria's head of state while waiting for my call to the beautician the day before. The official government language in Lagos is English, and I had no problem finding enough reading material. I had been impressed by the Christian tone in those speeches. One speech puzzled me. It had been given to the International Commission by the Nigerian head of state after the capitulation of Biafra.

"You have now seen with your own eyes that all the terrible accusations of war crimes and propaganda are not true," it said in that speech. "Please, tell the world that we are not savages but a Christian people who believe in forgiveness and reconciliation!"

I was very surprised. I couldn't remember ever hearing about such a commission or someone setting the Biafra story straight in the American news media. But it could easily be that I had just missed it; I often don't get to the news as I should.

As I listened to Comfort, I began to wonder—*did* the American press tell *all* of it? Did they report for *both* sides?

Comfort's husband was a Nigerian by birth. He was a man of few words and did much more listening than talking. That morning he entered our conversation several times.

"America had no business taking Biafra's side," he told me emphatically. "She also didn't play fair when she sent in Red Cross planes supposedly loaded with food but carrying guns instead."

I blinked hard. This was a Communist tactic and *not* the American way.

Comfort tried to smooth things over.

"Maybe America tried to help because they were misinformed," she said gently, "but her blunder is costing her plenty. Nigeria, in spite of the strong Christian influence, is very pro-Russia by now. Our upper class are sending their sons to Moscow for higher education. Nigeria's oil goes to the Communist countries, too."

I knew that Nigeria was the land of black gold, highest in oil production among the African nations. It was hard to understand why poverty and the cost of living could be so high. I asked Comfort's husband about it.

"It's a matter of time," he said. "The land must heal from the war. Corruption is hard to fight, too. The Africans had nothing for so long; they feel it's time they get at least their share. They have also become very race conscious and resentful toward the white people. The government gives no entry visa to any South African at the present time. They do not permit new missionaries to enter the land and give very few visiting visas to Americans. We were very surprised that you even got to come here."

"What will that do to the spreading of the Christian Gospel?" I asked.

"The Gospel *is* spreading like never before, even in former Biafra," Comfort said quietly. "It is spread mainly by native missionaries. As the Communist influence is increasing, so is the power of the Gospel. It seems symbolic of the whole African continent."

I thought about her words as we flew across North Africa. Which way would Africa go in the future?

I also tried to figure out why there was so much hostility in the world against America. I found a few answers after we had been in Switzerland a few days.

The first view of that land was breathtaking. I had flown into the Alps before, but the snow-capped grandeur and beauty of Switzerland was in such sharp contrast to the dry drabness of drought-plagued Africa that I just looked down and shed tears, I was so glad to see it.

Ann and I had never been in Geneva, and we enjoyed it there from the first moment. It wasn't only that we found hot showers, snow-white sheets, the shimmering Lake Geneva, and the panorama much to our liking. Geneva also has a most interesting conglomeration of races and people. We met the first handful the following day.

Of course, I got my hair done before we did anything else, and I was charged ten dollars again. This time I didn't mind; the girl at least knew what she was doing and I looked presentable.

I felt very nervous about meeting the first few people and wondered why we even had come to Geneva. We knew nobody there; we came because someone in America had sent us a letter and a check. I had spoken in California at some church function where I mentioned our upcoming trip. The lady in charge and her daughter in another church had contacted us afterward and asked if we would be willing to stop in Geneva and meet their relatives. They also sent a check to cover the extra costs. I replied that we would be willing to do that if God would direct us that way.

He obviously did! In spite of bullying attempts to get us into France or Rome (we knew and wanted to visit missionaries there!) we got a flight to Geneva.

Here we were, feeling very awkward about calling a total stranger and wondering when to leave again. That we had to leave soon was of no question; the hotel and food prices were such that we could stay only another night. Africa had wiped our budget clean. We could only "limp" home.

Phyllis sounded very warm and charming when I called the number given to me by her mother. She appeared to be even more charming when we got to her apartment. She had invited several of her friends, and within a short time we felt very much at home. Most of her friends had been born in America, as she had been. They had come to Switzerland because of marriage or job opportunity. Phyllis' husband was a successful Swiss businessman.

"How long will you stay?" someone asked.

"I do not know," I replied honestly. "I don't even know why we are here. I believe that God sent us here, but I have no idea for what reason. It depends very much on whether we can find a very cheap hotel somewhere. We cannot stay in the hotel we are now in; the prices are prohibitive for us at the end of our tour."

"You don't need to stay in *any* hotel," one of Phyllis' friends said. "I have a big house and a guest room with two beds. You are most welcome to stay with us!"

Margie sounded so sweet and genuine that we accepted her invitation and moved our luggage from the hotel to her beautiful, rambling country home. Was I ever glad that we did! We could come and go as we pleased. The bus stop was close, and we wandered to and fro as needed. Her refrigerator was at our disposal. We couldn't thank God enough for His kind and bountiful provision. As the days unfolded, I could see God's purpose for bringing us to Geneva.

First I visited the International Red Cross headquarters where I found an American official and asked him what could be done about wheelchairs for South Vietnam. The gentleman looked puzzled. "Nobody has told us about *that* need," he said. "We are shipping medications, food, and other materials in, but I have no request for wheelchairs!"

"I suppose that short-term needs are often so urgent that long-term solutions are neglected," I said. "If crippled people can move, they can make a living and then we won't have to feed them forever. What does a Chinese proverb say? 'Give someone a fish and he has a meal. Teach someone *how* to fish and he makes a living.'"

The man smiled at me. "I appreciate your concern and enthusiasm. Here is my card. Let's work together and see what we can do. I can promise this much already: If you can find some wheelchairs in the United States, we'll transport them without charge to Saigon." I thanked him and left.

"So far so good. What is next, Lord?" I asked.

We visited and were entertained at various places, and it gave me an insight into how Americans related in European countries. Most of them have found a happy balance between their unique American roots and the restrictions of European culture.

Phyllis, for instance, has a typical Swiss home. Her furniture and china, her silver and entertainment are of the sophisticated, European tradition, but she herself has never lost the free spirit of her American upbringing.

"Did you have a hard time adjusting to the life over here after you got married?" I asked her.

"Yes and no," she smiled. "I was a typical American teenager and life was one big lark for me. Luckily I am able to go back to the United States for a visit whenever things get to me over here."

Another American woman laughed as she listened, "You have lived on both sides, Hansi, and you can guess what is hardest for Americans to learn in Europe. It is to live without the American freedom. Even in the so-called 'free' countries there are so many restrictions, so much stuffiness! Even the Swiss themselves joke about it. They say they have only two alternatives: a thing is either forbidden or required!" I nodded; how well I understood.

Americans in other countries do not miss only that special portion of individual freedom that we in America take so much for granted; they also worry about America. That came home to me after I had been invited to speak in the International Church. I found myself in a conflict as I walked up to the pulpit that Sunday morning. I knew that the congregation consisted of American and European members. I was aware of the critical attitude among the latter toward the United States as a nation. I prayed for the right topic, and God said, "Speak about what you love most!"

I told the listeners a bit about my past and how I had found Jesus. I love Jesus most and I said so; but I love the United States, too, and I said that. I also told them what was *right* about my adopted country.

"I have two great loves in my new life," I said quietly, "my Lord and Master Jesus Christ, and my new homeland, America. God gave it to me so that I might know what it means to belong. In my own heart Jesus Christ and America belong together because . . ." The minister stood up and interrupted my sentence.

"Thank you very much," he said, visibly embarrassed, "we appreciate your testimony, but we must close." I blinked in disbelief. Wouldn't he at least let me finish my thought?

Couldn't I tell *why* I think of Christ and America as belonging together? Because America *is* preaching Christ as no other nation ever has. She built her foundation and precepts two hundred years ago on Christ's teachings.

No, he didn't let me finish. He closed the service in a formal way and invited everyone to a coffee hour in the back of the church. We went there. I felt horrible for Phyllis' sake. She had asked the minister to let me speak, and I didn't want to embarrass that dear woman. If she was embarrassed, she didn't show it. She was again a perfect church hostess, charming, warm, and thoughtful, and she saw to it that the visitors felt at home as she served coffee.

One woman came up to me. She had tears in her eyes.

"You'll never know what you did for me this morning," she said and cried some more. "I have lived in Switzerland for the last five years and have had no chance to visit America for that long. You are the first one who ever said anything good about America in all the five years I have lived here. Even the American newspapers say nothing but bad things. I had begun to wonder if there was *anything* good left over there."

I looked at my troubled fellow American and I ached for her. She, like thousands of others, had to depend on the news media to hear about their land. If *she* began to wonder if our nation was going rotten, what must our enemies think? Didn't they have reason to rejoice?

"Listen," I said to her, "there is *much* good left in America. The true and good Americans outnumber the bad and ugly Americans by a long shot. America is still doing what she has done for so long—helping others! I have just finished a world tour, and I have seen it with my own eyes. America is still the number one land of missions and a defender of freedom. I am glad to be a Christian, but I am also proud to be an

American! You should be, too!" She smiled through her tears and squeezed my hand.

A banker and his wife invited Ann and me for Sunday dinner. I had met the wife in the group Phyllis had introduced us to when we arrived. She had been a former American actress and was most vivacious and outspoken. Her husband had been born in America, too, but had by unusual circumstances found his way into the Swiss banking business.

"It isn't done very often," he smiled. "The Swiss don't let outsiders come into their banks. We came here so long ago that we managed to get our foot in."

"Are you an American or a Swiss citizen?" I asked.

"You can carry both citizenships in this land," the man said.

The family lived in one of those picturesque chalets that could have shown up on any travel poster about Switzerland. From the shutters to the windowboxes to the shingled roof, it had the authentic charm of a Swiss farmhouse. Inside it combined old-fashioned coziness with ultra-modern American gadgets. The house was a dream, and I said so.

Although the house was in Swiss style, the hospitality was American. Europeans are hospitable, too, but mostly to their friends. They are not in the habit of bringing strangers home for dinner. Every invitation we received anywhere while in Europe came from fellow Americans.

The dinner was delicious, and the conversation was very lively from the beginning. The banker seemed plainly amused by my spirited defense of America.

"Hansi," he finally said and smiled a patient little smile, "it is refreshing to hear someone like you go to bat for America, but America is on her way out."

"Why would you say that, sir?" I asked and felt very defensive.

"I have the finger on the pulse of the world so far as it concerns finances," he said seriously, "and I know that the American dollar is in trouble!"

That the dollar was in trouble I could tell for myself. Every time we exchanged our travelers checks in any land for foreign money, it seemed to pay for less and less. Switzerland seemed worse than any other place except Nigeria. I didn't answer, I just listened as he continued.

"As a matter of fact, it is inevitable that the dollar will crash. We expect it to do so within the next twelve to fifteen months."

My mind boggled at what I had just heard. Did he say months or years?

"Twelve to fifteen months," he repeated, "if it takes that long."

I swallowed hard and tried to comprehend the magnitude of such a national crisis. It would bring chaos, riots, lawlessness in such a dimension that I couldn't even imagine it. That seemed bad enough, but the thing that bothered me the most was something entirely different. If the dollar lost its buying power or even died altogether, who would feed the thousands of hungry children around the globe?

Jim's organization alone fed nearly 80,000 of them every month through their foster parent program. Eighty thousand Americans provided dollars for food, letters, and prayers to those unfortunate kids they had never seen in their lives. What would happen to the thousands of mission compounds around the world if the dollar crashed? How many lights of hope would go out on this earth if the American people had nothing left to give? I shook my head and looked that Swiss-American financier straight in the eyes.

"I don't understand politics and money at all," I told him and took a very deep breath. "All I know is that I pray you are wrong. God's message must be preached to all the world. Who will do it if America goes under? I can't believe that God will forsake America as long as we do His bidding. I have to believe that your prediction will not come true as soon as you say!"

The man was as sober as I when he answered.

"Hansi, I didn't give you a prediction, I gave you a fact. America *is* already bankrupt. When the dollar crashes, the whole world will suffer."

His wife added, "We can see the handwriting on the wall. We here in Switzerland do the only sensible thing we can do. We store up like the squirrels for the winter."

I knew what she meant. I had seen the gold bars under heavy glass the last time I had gone to a bank to exchange more dollars for Swiss francs. The price of one small gold bar sounded incredible to me.

I knew I would never buy any gold and silver. If we had any money, we would send it out as fast as possible to help someone. At least I wouldn't have to mourn for my lost treasures when the crash came. I also wondered if she had ever read the text in the Old Testament about people throwing their silver and gold away. (*See* Ezekiel 7:19.)

I was glad they felt they could store up for hard times. As for me, I know what I must do! Go back to America as fast as possible and send every dollar out while it still could do a work for God. I couldn't wait to go home!

27
Is There a Special Story?

Although I was eager to leave, God had a few more errands for me to run. One was a speaking appointment for a women's luncheon. Most of the ladies had been at the worship service, and I was treated by several European ladies rather icily, to say the least. I spoke to them about the key to healing, which is forgiveness. I shared how Corrie ten Boom had been used by God to heal my collective guilt about Nazi concentration camps.(See *Hansi's New Life*, 1975.) I asked at the end of the meeting if any of my sisters in that circle needed to forgive and be healed also. I prayed a short prayer about forgiveness and left right afterward because I had to meet someone for an interview.

Phyllis told me later what happened after I had gone. God spoke to many hearts that noon and many realized for the first time how many grudges they carried against each other, against other nationalities, against Germans especially!

I met the following day in a private home for a prayer meeting with some of the same ladies. God began much healing that day. Wrong attitudes and bitterness were confessed, questions were answered, and Christ became more real to all of us.

"I am so glad God and my mother sent you to Geneva," Phyllis said to me before we had to leave. "God has begun something in our church that was needed. I just pray and hope that it will grow. Prejudice and resentments can keep so many blessings away. There is so much to do for us Christians in this sophisticated city and all over Switzerland. This land needs a new revelation of Jesus Christ!"

I wasn't so sure that her minister thought the same way. I met with him for lunch in one of the employee cafeterias of a well-known international Christian organization where he had been a key figure before accepting a parish call. It was obvious that he didn't quite know what to do with me. I didn't waste time with small talk.

"How do *you* feel about your relationship with America?" I asked him.

He hesitated. "I see myself much more as a citizen of the whole world than as an American," he said hesitatingly. "My wife is different; she was born of missionary parents in China and her sense of belonging, her patriotism, are very clear. She feels much as you do."

"When you think of America as a nation, what comes to your mind?" I inquired.

"America as a nation has attempted what no other nation ever tried to do. Our forefathers tried to give their future generations a freedom nobody ever had before. They tried for equal opportunity, for justice, for help, and for love. Of course, there have been many shortcomings."

I looked at him. "What are your hopes for the future?"

"A world brotherhood of men," he said.

"How will you accomplish that with the aggression and threat of Communism on the other side?" I asked quietly.

He shrugged his shoulders. "It will take patience, endurance, and long suffering. Someday people will see that it is better to work together."

I thanked the clergyman and left. I had just gotten another answer to something else that puzzled me. I had read in one of the American Christian magazines an article that bemoaned the fact that American leaders in *any* international organization do not speak up any more. Strangely enough, America usually ends up paying most of the bills, be it at the UN or any other council—but other than that they are seldom heard. Representatives of any little nation of the third world or the countries friendly to Communism will stand up and criticize and denounce the United States about everything, and the United States delegates in world organizations sit there and take it all without protest. The magazine asked a pointed question: *What are we trying to prove by it?*

The interview with the American minister gave me the answer. Maybe some of our American representatives consider it the noble self-control of a superpower who has dreams of a world government?

The whole thing left me deeply disturbed, and I talked with Margie about it. Her father had been a well-known American who had come to Europe with the Marshall Plan. I read some of the papers he had written. He was Chief of Mission in Greece and in Belgium in 1948 to 1950. He presented his views in a paper at a conference sponsored by the Federation of Theological Schools at a well-known university in 1958.

Some of his statements I read showed that the struggle of the cold war had begun long before I had been aware of it. Margie's father is now dead, but it would be well if America listened even today to his advice. The cold war isn't over, and it will not go away by ignoring it. I quote just a small portion:

> This contest which we call the Cold War has been fought with intensity for the past dozen years, but we cannot within the limits of our time review much of the past. However, we might start with a synopsis of the previous chapters as it is reflected by the present score in terms of population. There are approximately 400 million people in the Christian or Free World and double this amount, 800 million, in the Communist World. What is frequently lost sight of is that there are as many people as these two amounts put together, namely 1 billion 200 million, in the rest of the world—the Uncommitted World.
>
> It should be quite obvious that these 1 billion 200 million people in the uncommitted nations are the balance of power in this world struggle and will ultimately tip the scales one way or the other. These uncommitted nations comprise almost entirely the underdeveloped nations. This great world contest today, therefore, is a struggle for the allegiance of these underdeveloped nations. That there is a military build-up in the background, which cannot be disregarded, is important, but the crux of the contest, I repeat, is the allegiance of the underdeveloped nations.

Do Americans think that they can win the third world by passive silence, by having no opinions of their own left?

Why Americans think that silence and taking every abuse is *always* good puzzles greater heads than mine, I found out! One lady who is very active in the American community of Geneva asked me a strange question.

"How much do you know about Solzhenitsyn?"

"Not too much, I have to admit," I answered.

"Do you know that he has left Russia and is traveling abroad?" she challenged me.

"I heard about it between countries," I laughed. "I haven't seen an American newspaper for many weeks."

"Since you live in the United States, do you think it could be true what Solzhenitsyn's secretary said to me? I went to a lecture recently and met a man who claims to be just that. He told me that Solzhenitsyn lost his honeymoon with the American press before it even began."

"Why is that?" I decided to be cautious and just listen! (Oh, how American I can be!)

"Well, Solzhenitsyn had a press conference, and he asked the American news people a very embarrassing question. 'How is it,' he supposedly asked, 'that the American news media roars like a fearless lion at home but abroad and about the socialistic countries they behave like timid little lambs?'

"The press didn't print his question," the woman continued, "but from that day on the American news media tried either to ignore him or to call him an unrealistic dreamer who saw things *too* simply to fit into a complex Western world. Do you think the American press could do such a thing?"

"I don't want to believe it," I said to her, "but I am afraid I will have to do a bit of close listening when I return home. I heard several things on my world tour that I hadn't thought possible. I just hope we still have a 'free' press in America."

If God had used me to bring a bit of peace and reassurance to some of my fellow Americans in Geneva, I left the place with several new, disturbing questions in my heart. I knew I would have to give various things at home a closer look.

Before I could do that, however, we had one more stop to make. I promised Bill and Harriet that we would try to stop at his mission house in Austria.

I had met both a few months before in California while they were home on furlough. Their work was very close to my heart. Bill had been sent to Europe twenty years ago as an evangelist. He and Harriet had served Central Europe with the spreading of the Gospel and had made occasional visits into the East-bloc countries. One minister behind the Iron Curtain had asked Bill during one of his tourist visits: "What is your work, my brother?"

"I am an evangelist for Jesus Christ," Bill answered.

"If that is your calling, please do not forget that our land needs evangelizing, too. Do not stop just because you see a closed door. Try it and see if it is locked!"

Bill and his wife took that as a special message from God and from that moment concentrated their special efforts on the countries behind the Iron Curtain.

When we got to Austria, we found that Bill and Harriet had a place that could receive many "guests." These people were actually teams who received special training in how to take Bibles into the Communist world. Bill himself, with his family, went East as often as possible to preach and strengthen the believers.

From the outside nobody could guess what a special place that house was. It looked like a typical Austrian pension, of which Austria has hundreds. Harriet spoke a fluent German. I could sense a special spirit in the place the moment we entered. In addition to Bill and his family, we found a couple from another European country and two young girls to be the staff. The young women were from America, too, and they worked without pay. The whole project was very much a faith project.

Prayer undergirded their work. The very first day we spent with them began with a prayer meeting. Everyone present received a stack of little cards. On most of them was a picture and the name of a person. Besides birth date and nationality, sentences read: "In prison for five years; all property confiscated"; "hard labor camp for seven years"; "imprisoned for two years. Family in urgent need." I read card after card in my little stack, and my eyes burned like my heart.

First we all prayed silently for all the names, then we took turns praying out loud. As I listened to the prayers of the staff, I noticed that two extra names came up in everyone's prayers. One name was Joseph, the other Vasile. Bill's secretary broke down and cried as she mentioned him. After the prayer service was over, I looked for Bill.

"Is there a special story behind these two names?" I asked that kind, dedicated man.

"There surely is," he said solemnly, "sit down and I'll tell you about it.

"Joseph is the modern Martin Luther of Rumania. The Reformation never reached the South European countries, as you might know. Right now they have *their* reformation. It began when Joseph returned from his studies in London and realized that his church was slowly being strangled by socialistic elements. The whole process and how it is done is devilish.

"The laws of every Eastern land give every citizen freedom of worship. You see, the Western world gets pretty confused about Christian freedom behind the Iron Curtain. One person claims the church is totally underground; others claim that they have religious freedom. The truth is in the middle.

"The churches exist, but the leading body is often infiltrated by Communist informers or hirelings, who will never give *any* written or printed orders. Every limitation or threat contrary to the laws of the land are given verbally. When they try to cut worship services out or try to stop the forming of youth groups or do anything else that could stop the growth of churches, they *say:* 'You had better not or you'll be in for trouble.' So the churches are persecuted but have no evidence to show or prove anything with.

"Joseph wrote and circulated a paper pointing out the difficulties and challenging the Christians to ask for their legal rights. It hit like a bombshell and woke up the believers of various denominations. The churches began to come alive.

"Next, Joseph wrote and printed a second paper for the Communists. He sent one of them right to the head of state. In that paper he shows first of all why Marxism makes atheists out of people.

"To create a bloody revolution, the Communists have to create bitter, discontented, angry men. Christianity wouldn't serve their purpose too well.

" 'You have achieved your goal,' he said in his little booklet. 'I am not here to topple the socialistic government or fight the state. I want to show you *how* you can change your angry, discontented men back into constructive, positive members of society.'

"Joseph then quoted some findings and statistics the Reds had as a top secret; juvenile delinquency is soaring sky high in the cities of Communist countries, too. It is seldom mentioned or acknowledged publicly; nevertheless, the problems are very real. In an investigation the Communists found out to their great surprise that Christian youth groups in their lands had *no* juvenile delinquency at all. Joseph challenged his Communist government to try the Christian model and see what it would do for the land.

"A few days after the paper had been sent, Joseph heard a knock on the door. Seven men of the secret police entered and searched his little apartment. They searched the three little rooms for eight hours and confiscated his library, tape recorder, tapes, sermon notes, and everything in print or in writing.

"They couldn't find any evidence to substantiate their claim that he was plotting against the heads of state, so they began to interrogate him from day to day."

At the time Bill told me about it, Joseph was still under daily interrogation but had not gone to prison yet. No wonder the staff had pleaded so fervently for that man.

"What about Vasile?" I asked Bill.

"He is already in prison because he gave some fellow Christians Bibles. He was the right hand of Joseph and very dedicated.

"We had left a whole load of Bibles with him the last time we visited in Bucharest. One brother came and picked up some Bibles. On his way home a general search of every suitcase brought the Bibles to the attention of the police. It was only a matter of time before they forced the frightened man to confess the source of his Bibles and Vasile went straight to jail for spreading Western literature.

"That isn't our greatest sorrow. Many believers are in jail. None of them is accused for his religious conviction, however, but for something that can be applied to the laws of the land. So we pray for them, take money in to keep their families from starving, and stand by in any way we can.

"Our great heartbreak is that Vasile has turned against us Christians.

His wife is permitted to visit him every month for fifteen minutes. He told her that he didn't want to hear a thing about Christianity; he was finished with it. The Communists had produced some documents with Joseph's signature. In it they proved to Vasile that he had been betrayed by Joseph. It turned Vasile bitter.

"We have made a study of it. We wondered why some of our believers give in to the Communist pressure and brainwashing while others stand firm. I think we have found the answer." Bill paused and reflected.

I looked at him and held my breath. Did that man *know* how much I had wondered about just that, especially on my world tour? Whenever I had found myself in the reach of Communism and the possibility that we could be captured, I had begun to ask myself the same question: Could anyone brainwash me again? Would I stay true to Jesus Christ no matter what they did to me? How could I know that I couldn't be deceived again?

"Joseph and Vasile are a typical example of what we found," Bill said emphatically. ·

"A believer who keeps his eyes on Jesus cannot be moved. Joseph is proving that point. They are interrogating him as much as twelve to fifteen hours a day. That is absolute torture to anybody's brain. It is a deadly cat-and-mouse game and wears a person down *more* than imprisonment. But Joseph is holding up. I visited him just a few days ago and recorded an interview. We smuggled the tape out, and I want you to listen to it. Joseph is ready for prison and torture for Christ.

"Vasile, on the other hand, kept his eyes on man. He was a deep admirer of Joseph and followed a human leader. Regardless of how great or good a person is, trust in another human being *can* be shaken. The Communists fabricated lies about Joseph, and Vasile believed them. They could not have lied about Jesus Christ to him. So it is in many cases. The devil is a master of lying and falsehood. He will smear any child of God. If people look at other people, they build their faith on drifting sand. If they keep their eyes on Jesus, *nobody* can get to them."

"Thank You, Lord," I said and tears began to roll. Bill didn't know what he had just done for me. His words had taken a nagging worry out of my heart, a fear that I perhaps had carried in me ever since I had found the Lord.

I was so afraid of brainwashing because I knew the devilish subtlety of it. I had wondered if anyone could ever again turn me against truth. Now I had found the answer and peace flooded my heart. It sounded so simple and yet it was special, real and great: Keep your eyes on Jesus *alone!*

28
Like the Troubled Sea

We formed another prayer circle that morning and prayed once more for Vasile. God gave us sweet assurance right then and there. Vasile would find his way again and learn from it.

Bill taped several interviews with me for his weekly radio broadcast in the States. Of course he never used his real name in public. It would have cost him his chance to go into the Eastern countries.

One land had closed to him just recently, anyhow: Czechoslovakia. I just sat and cried some more when he told me how it happened. He loved the believers in my former homeland in a special way and spent much time in Prague and other places. He didn't even need to smuggle too many Bibles in; they had ways of printing them right there if they had enough money to pay for the paper and the labor. He saw to it that they got what was needed.

A minister from the free world contacted him one day and asked if he would take some printed material for the believers of another denomination into Prague with him. Bill consented and had a strange foreboding about the whole deal.

The very next time he tried to go into Czechoslovakia, he was held at the border, questioned for several hours, and finally denied entry as an "undesirable" visitor for Czechoslovakia.

Bill was sure it had something to do with that request he had felt so uneasy about. He wrote to that minister and asked if he had written anything behind the Iron Curtain. When the answer came, he couldn't believe his eyes. The man verified that he had written a letter into Czechoslovakia! He had announced Bill's coming by his *real name* to his friends in Prague and told them to look for him for Bill would bring printed material in to them.

Bill looked at me and he had agony in his eyes.

"That one letter, opened and registered by the Communist authorities, put me on their black list. Why would a Christian man be *that* ignorant? Why would he repay my willingness to do him a favor by giving us such unnecessary troubles?"

"Some people are so naive, maybe even stupid, that they cannot comprehend the Communist system," I said. "They believe that by acting as if everything were all right they can make it all right."

Bill nodded. "You are right. Some American organizations operate under that assumption. A well-known Bible society whose president is convinced that Communists can be dealt with if just approached *right*, contacted Rumania's government for a special deal. He offered to send paper and to pay for the printing of several thousand testaments. The Communists agreed readily to do as told. They took the money and announced openly in the Communist newspapers that anyone who wanted a Bible could register with them and pay for it (even though it already had been paid for!). Several hundred Christians dared to do it in spite of knowing they were disclosing their identify. They were providing the Communists with a free list and addresses of people the Reds were looking for—they wanted a Bible that much!

"Then the authorities *did* print the Bibles as agreed—in an archaic print and language that only a few very old people are still able to read and understand.

"As soon as it was known, our believers backed out. Why pay for something they couldn't read? The Communists took pictures of the stacks of Bibles that were not claimed by anybody, trying to prove by it that the Rumanian people had no need or interest in such books."

I shook my head. I began to understand the advice of Jesus: "Be wise as serpents and harmless as doves." (See Matthew 10:16.)

"Bill, how is it that we hear at one time that the churches are growing and things are doing better, and maybe just a month later we hear about grave persecution in some parts of the Communist world. Is there such a thing as the 'underground church'?"

"The Bible says that the wicked are like the troubled sea," Bill said very deliberately. "I cannot think of any description that could describe the Communists better. They are without peace, relentless, and everything comes and goes in waves. They operate by oppression and fear to unnerve people because the Reds can never be predicted.

"Today they torture, tomorrow they sit back and watch. *Underground church* is not the right word for the situation. *The persecuted church* is the better definition. Sure, there are some groups in hiding, especially in Russia where a church cannot be founded unless they have a certain number of members. So the small groups have to meet privately and in secret. They are often interdenominational because doctrinal differences become insignificant in times of persecution.

"It all becomes very simple in the end. People believe in Jesus Christ and are persecuted, or they deny His name and are okay. So they call themselves not Baptists or Lutherans or Methodists, but 'believers.' Believers in Jesus Christ."

I understood what Bill was saying. I had known for a long time that the enemy of God will always fight one name only: Jesus Christ.

The devil doesn't mind if people believe in a god. The Nazis never took my faith in God away when I was brainwashed. They only undermined my faith in the Jew, Jesus Christ. The devil believes what the Bible says, "For there is none other name under heaven given among men, whereby we must be saved" (Acts 4:12).

The Communists know that, too. They treat people who believe in that name as political enemies. They know that the Christian ethic has *nothing* in common with their philosophy, and they want to wipe it out.

"You see," Bill explained, "if Communism would have a uniform pressure of persecution at all times, the church would go underground and be much harder to find. So the Reds relax things after a while. The Christians thank God, rejoice, and come out of hiding. The Communists sit and watch and take notes. Then out of the blue sky, it seems, they attack again and begin to *clean up.*"

"Bill, when you or the teams that you are training go in, is there acute danger for your life?"

Bill nodded. "Yes, anyone involved in this work takes risks. We are aware that our United States citizenship does not necessarily protect us from imprisonment or *accidental* death. Keep one thing in mind, however—we are no heroes. We are not very brave, nor are we afraid. We trust God! We know that the fear of suffering is often worse than suffering itself. Our great concern is not only our own safety but the welfare of the believers we leave behind.

"When we train and pick people for teams, we keep that uppermost in our minds. You see, there are many Americans who are ever so sincere and eager to work with us. They come here and are ready to go in. If we'd let them go, they would do many indiscreet things behind the Iron Curtain. They would come back ever so proudly and be celebrated as Christian heroes in their American churches while our believers, meanwhile, would have been taken to jail by the Communists."

I nodded; I had an idea what he meant. Americans in general can be so naive, unsuspecting—and loud.

Bill continued, "Lenin knew Christians quite well. He wrote, 'Religious people are the most *gullible* people.' He knew what he was talking about; he had two years' training in a Christian seminary. Marx, a Jew by birth, supposedly was at one time close to Christian conversion, too. Somewhere along the way both Lenin and Marx got disillusioned about religion and turned against it. What a loss for Christ's cause!

"Our greatest mistake is to underestimate the enemies of God. They are highly intelligent, highly motivated, efficient, capable, and well educated. God knows what He is trying to tell us when He says in the Bible, 'For the children of this world are in their generation wiser than the children of light' (Luke 16:8).

"We here at our mission have a special theme, 'Whatsoever your hands find to do, do it *mightily.*' God deserves quality work!

"We try to understand the other side first, in order to match Satan's devices. After all, we *do* have the greater power on our side to help and guide us in our thinking and doing. We also have to depend on the Holy Spirit whenever we come to the end of our own resources.

"Picture yourself, for instance, as a member of our Bible teams. All you have—not written down, mind you, but in your memory—is a name of a believer and the name of a village. There are numerous villages in Communist lands that are not on the map, have no named or marked streets, and no numbers on the houses.

"Our teams go to such places to make contact. They have orders not to make any inquiries, not to draw *any* attention to themselves, not to wake up any dogs if they arrive at night, not to click any heels (one loud shoe could be a disaster).

"We don't send people who can't pray or be guided by the Holy Spirit. We know wherever God guides, He provides. We could write books about the miracles God has done for us.

"I am thinking of one family who had never seen any of us. God showed them in a dream that we were coming. As we drove slowly through the streets wondering where the family lived, a door suddenly opened and somebody motioned quietly. We stopped and stepped into the house, without a word. We were welcomed with tears and rejoicing; the people *knew* our faces already and had been waiting for us."

As I listened to Bill, I thought of an incident that had taken place in America before I went on tour. I had spoken at a church gathering and told some stories about the happenings behind the Iron Curtain. (I had used our family tithing money for years, even before the Hansi Ministries came into being, to provide help to our believers in Communist lands.) I knew many stories through letters and special visits I had received. After all, some of my own people were involved in that struggle.

One of the great immediate objectives of our new corporation was to provide more and better aid to such projects. It was one of the reasons why we visited Bill's place. I wanted to see with my own eyes if and how we should help. I also wanted to know if the stories I had related in the past were really true. They were! I heard and learned a lot more that I could tell after I would return to America. I also found some answers I had not been able to give in the past.

I'll never forget an American doctor who pushed himself through the crowd one afternoon following one of my services. He was obviously very well-to-do, he was religious, and he let me know that he was head elder in his church. He was very self-assured, too!

"Now tell me," he said, and his bushy eyebrows folded into a big frown, "if your stories are true and our believers *are* in need of Bibles and material help, why is it that they don't accept help when it is offered to them?"

He glared at me and said, "I visited Moscow just last summer, and I even found a church in which to worship. At the end I offered someone in the audience my Bible. I also took my coat off and handed it to a man of similar size. Both were refused. The minister came to me and seemed very offended. He said in English: 'We don't need your gifts. We are a happy and contented people who have everything we need. Please, leave us alone.' So I took my coat and Bible and left."

I had a pretty good idea how to explain it to the doctor, but I didn't dare say too much, at least not then. I had heard so many conflicting stories, I wasn't sure any more of anything. I wanted to tell him then and there that if for no other reason his gifts had been refused because he had acted without tact.

Americans forget so often when they act in the role of the wealthy benefactor that even the poorest human being longs for dignity. Nobody is ever so down and out that he wants to be treated like a dog who waits for crumbs. It always creates resentment. Americans as a whole are never heartless, but they can be *so* thoughtless, even when they try to help. I have observed that often.

I still remember when church people would drop things off at my house, first to help us as we tried to make a new beginning and later so that we could send them to the mission fields. They would give us dirty, torn, broken things that couldn't be repaired even if we had tried to do so. Not all of it was bad, of course; we got good stuff, too, and used it for years.

If Americans could only remember: Treat others as you want to be treated. Give only what you would use yourself. Give your handouts with the same tact you would hope for if you were in the same place.

How would that American doctor have felt if a Communist had walked into his church some day and offered him, in the presence of the whole congregation, the coat off his back?

Furthermore, after I talked to Bill, I knew that if anyone in that church in Moscow had accepted the doctor's gift, he would have jeopardized himself gravely.

Any "open" church worship behind the Iron Curtain has Communist informers and government spies in attendance. Every believer knows that. Some ministers are wolves in sheepskin, disguised Communist agents who serve an "open" church to prove to the world that socialistic countries *do* have religious freedom. Believers can never feel safe, sometimes not even in their own homes. Many parents have been betrayed by their own children. Young people are constantly under the influence of atheists and educators who tell them it is their duty to report anyone who opposes socialistic progress.

"Hansi," Bill said, after we talked for a long time about the ideology of Communism (and I found him to be a well-read, thorough researcher who avoided generalizations and clichés carefully), "our ultimate enemy is not Communism, it is Satan. We don't even contend with human flesh but with superpowers under heaven.

"I look with great concern at American politics of the last few years. Our American leaders do not see the whole picture. They cannot see it in the right perspective either, or perhaps they don't *want* to see it. If you read what Lenin wrote as early as in the 1920s, the Communists' goals are clear. You can follow their thinking. The Communists *know* what they are doing, and they plan to reach their ultimate goal: to make the whole world Communist.

"Lenin laid it out. First get Asia. Neutralize Europe; then isolate America from the rest of the world. After that America will fall under the same dictatorship by inner decay and without the use of destructive weapons."

"Wasn't Lenin afraid that America's Christian philosophy would hold back the tide of atheism?" I interrupted Bill.

"Why should he have been?" Bill answered. "The Russian churches were no fortress against the tide of evil and the revolution. If Lenin were alive today, he would just sneer about Western religion. We might be more sophisticated than the orthodox Russian church was, but we are just as lethargic."

I swallowed hard. It was so hard for me to think of America as a target for Communism. Bill continued his trend of thought.

"Hansi, we here in Europe can feel the pulse of the world from both sides. We do painstaking research for our broadcasts; we can substantiate every statement we make. I am afraid that Cambodia and Vietnam will fall before the year is over, and Thailand and South Korea and some other countries will before long be in deep trouble."

"I hope you are wrong," I said and stood up. "Bill, I can't even discuss the possibility that Cambodia could fall. I told you about my orphans there. I believe with all my heart that God will perform a miracle. It cannot happen, not now! The Gospel is spreading. God will not let our enemies stop His work!"

I was so upset, I just had to go away for a while. I could hardly stand to think about what Bill had said.

"Remember, sometimes God uses the wicked as a sword to bring His children to repentance," Bill had also said as I walked out the door for a walk. "Remember. . . ."

Evening dusk was around me. I stood and looked at the fading sky and watched the tips of the Alps glow in the golden fire of a setting sun.

"God," I prayed, "give me the courage to face what You want to teach me. Show me what to do. Bless us all—and bless this mission and Bill and all who work here. Most of all, be near those who are in bondage for You."

29
Two Thousand Tongues to Go!

If God's children only knew what even little prayers can do! If we only knew what God wants to do *through* our simple prayers. He has limited Himself to a spiritual law that we must *ask* first and *then* He will act. The question that our believers in Communist countries ask their Western visitors first and most often is: "Do you pray for us?"

"We do pray much here at our mission for our suffering brothers and sisters in Christ," Harriet said. "It is so often the only thing we can do when we cannot be with them in their troubles.

"Lately I have begun to fast at least one day a week. It gives me a deeper compassion for the families who are left in dire need when the breadwinner goes to prison for his faith. The authorities will deliberately let the family go hungry and make sure that the head of the home knows about it. Nothing tends to break the human spirit more than when a parent knows that his child is hurting."

"Even though they have so many cares of their own," another staff member said, "the believers remember always to pray for us and for America!"

I hung my head in shame. How much does America pray for them, I asked myself. We Americans keep ourselves so busy we have often no time to pray at all. Some church people are too religious to have room for Christ and His compassion.

Bill showed me a list of the questions he always asks American Christians when he speaks to them:

1. What would you do if capture comes before rapture in America?

2. If you were ever put in jail for being a Christian, would your enemies find enough proof of your Christianity to convict you?

3. If your enemies were to take your Bibles away from you *now,* how much and what do you have stored away within you of God's Word?

4. If your children were taken away from your home now, how *much* would they know and remember about the Christian faith?

I thought about that list during the long flight hours after we finally boarded the plane in London for our last stretch home.

Harriet had taken us to their airport. We hated to part; our friendship had become within a week so deep that we knew it was cemented for eternity. Bill had shared so much of himself and his deep insights. I had learned a lot. We also spent time together to see the beauty of God's handiwork. Austria is so similar to Switzerland in beauty and culture; it never fails to inspire me. God even gave me a chance to speak to American GIs in Austria during that week. What a good time we had! I enjoyed it as much as I did my time with our boys in Korea!

It was so good to be on the way home. As much as I love to travel, I always carry a deep homesickness in me until my feet touch American ground again. I wondered if it was the length of time I had been away that made me so excited when the plane set down in Seattle. After all, seven weeks in which we saw three continents and fourteen countries can seem like a very long time. I was so happy I almost hugged the American customs officer. I also addressed him in German because I couldn't remember anymore which language belonged where. I was so tired. Would homecoming to America *always* be so special to me or only after world tours?

I found out that I felt exactly the same way months later when I returned after a ten-day trip to Mexico. I had gone there because I knew that I had to meet one more group of true Americans. I had heard about them in South Vietnam for the first time. What I heard sounded so incredible that I had made a mental note to check further into it. I am glad I visited the Bible translators in the interior of Southern Mexico *after* my world tour, otherwise the whole experience could have been too overwhelming.

I visited the impressive headquarters of the organization in Mexico City and asked the regional director many questions.

Where did it all start? The whole big operation started with a skinny, sickly young American who later would be known as "Uncle Cam." His parents wanted him to be a minister in America, but he had a bent toward foreign missions. "The greater need is where the greatest darkness is," he said and landed only three years after high school graduation in Guatemala as a Bible salesman. The missionaries there gave him one superior look and said, "That scrawny fellow won't last two months!"

Cam surprised them all. He not only lasted and sold Bibles for a year; he decided to live with his young wife among the Cakchiquel Indians, learn their language, and translate the New Testament into their language.

Within ten years that tribe had the Scripture in their mother tongue, a school for children, a school for preachers, an orphanage, and a cooperative.

After that, Cam moved on. He couldn't forget how many more Bibleless tribes with no written language existed all over Central and South America—and all over the world. He decided to start a summer training school for anyone who wanted to learn an unwritten language. He knew he couldn't do it all alone anymore. He needed more Bible translators.

The kind of determination and faith Cam had was apparent when he started his first Summer Training Camp for Prospective Bible Translators in 1934 when the economic outlook in America was next to hopeless. The United States was still in the grip of the depression. Some Christian schools had closed down, and many congregations had lost their church buildings through mortgage foreclosure.

Cam had no money, no campus, no faculty, no students—and his wife had become a semi-invalid. Someone offered him an abandoned barn in Arkansas. A friend and Cam worked up a catalog to recruit students. By the time their first two full-time students arrived, they had even found an abandoned farmhouse to house the school in place of the old barn.

Thus started the now-largest linguistic organization in the world. Since 1935 their translators have reduced to writing more than 500 languages, many of them previously unknown. They have translated portions of the Bible and other literature into most of these languages and have taught many illiterate tribespeople to read.

Cam's vision has never stopped. He was one of the first to see the possibilities of the airplane for missionary work among remote jungle tribes. He used aviation and radio to conquer the mountains for Christ.

"We still work with the same philosophy Uncle Cam had," John, the director for Mexico, said to me. "We work with all denominations who want to work with us; we plan first and worry about the money later. We know that God provides if we are faithful and stay true to our calling!"

"Is Uncle Cam still alive?" I asked.

"Yes," I was told, "he is back in America, seventy-nine years young, still going strong, working hard toward the day when every tribe will know the Gospel."

I learned to love the translators deeply. God used me to speak to them and their families in several places. I also had a chance to visit some remote Indian villages high up in the rain forests of Southern Mexico. A trip by foot would have taken many days. The mission plane took us in within hours.

One visit I will never forget. I had asked to see a special project I had heard about. The young American translator, another Jim, and his wife, Nadine, were at the language center in Mitla when I met them. They had come in from their remote village for a training session. Their two small daughters enjoyed going to kindergarten and school for a change. In the village they were taught by their mother.

Jim was a former Texas farm boy and a seminary graduate. They had come to Mexico to live with the Lealao Chinantec people who lived far up in the valleys of some very rugged mountains. The young American family had spent nearly five years with "their" tribe already. Jim spoke the Indian language fluently. That particular language is one of the most difficult tonal languages possible. A one-syllable word can be given up to nine meanings merely by changing the pitch of the voice.

Jim had two great goals. His primary job was to translate God's Word into this difficult Indian language. His other goal? To help "his" tribe grow more corn in the mountainous forest to reduce the poverty and famine among them.

For centuries these Chinantecs have known only one traditional hit-or-miss farming method. There is little flatland there. The Indians must find for their fields slopes that are not so steep that people cannot stand on them without tumbling. Many have fallen to their death planting or harvesting in the past.

The Indians get the field ready by cutting down trees and bushes and then setting a torch to it. Into the ashes, every three feet, they plant four kernels of corn. Then they depend on fate and the weather for a harvest.

During the growing season torrents of summer rains fall, and the topsoil will be washed away because the fire will have exposed the land. Some corn may or may not grow into maturity. At best, the Chinantec farmers harvest about twenty pounds of corn for every pound that is planted. Some summers Jim watched the tribespeople live at the edge of starvation. Corn had to be flown in to keep the people alive.

"The pilot got tired of it and I got tired of it," Jim laughed. "I knew there ought to be a better and easier way to get more corn to the Chinantec than flying it in!"

I understood what he meant when we finally landed. We had come in over countless mountains, and the scenery had changed from the brown of the dry desert in Mitla to the deep, dark green of the heavy jungle growth.

The mission aviator, Jim, Tom (a young, newly converted Christian with a fine camera who took pictures for me), and I were all who could fit into the mission plane.

When the pilot got ready to land, I stretched my neck to see the landing strip. I could see nothing. The man at the controls searched the mountains carefully with his eyes; then he nodded. He flew several circles and set the nose of the little aircraft right against the side of a high mountain.

I held my breath. I finally saw a tiny light, green stripe, but it went straight up! That's how we landed, too—going straight up a mountain. We climbed a bit dazed out of the plane.

"Why did you circle?" I asked the missionary. "Couldn't you find the landing place?"

"I know how to find this place in my sleep," he laughed, "I have landed here so often. But I always make doubly sure that no wild animal

or person is on the runway. The strip is so narrow I would have no way
to avoid any obstacle, and it takes only one mistake to crash a plane."
    I looked around. The jungle edged the slim, steep, smooth slope on
all four sides. "We are constantly working on it to keep the runway
open," Jim said. "The rain forest takes over almost in an instant if we
don't watch it. We worked for years to get this strip cleared and ready.
Before we were able to land here, we landed two mountains over, and
my family and I had a day's walk in order to get in and out."
    "How did you do it when your daughters were so small?" I asked.
    "We carried them; we didn't mind except in emergencies," he con-
tinued. "Then things could get very bad, but God has never let us
down."
    The sweat began to pour down our faces. We followed Jim on a tiny
serpentine trail down the mountain toward the village. We went past
it to go to his project, which took us back up another mountain. Jim had
begun to teach his tribe how to grow corn on mountain terraces.
    Fifteen years ago an energetic Englishman named David had tried to
teach the Tzeltal tribe the same thing. The Tzeltal people live several
hundred miles east of the Chinantecs, and they had laughed about the
white man's suggestions.
    "Build ridges like steps in your mountain fields and plant the corn on
the flat part. Bring chicken manure and enrich your soil. It helps corn
to grow better."
    It sounded so stupid to them!
    Only *one* Tzeltal, who was a Christian, had the courage to try the
white man's method. For two years his crops failed, and he was the
laughing stock of the tribe. The third year that simple tribesman asked
God to make the plants grow so that his neighbors could be convinced
of a better way. God answered the prayer. Harvest was a victory! The
praying man's beans were ten times more prolific than those of the
others; his ears of corn were almost twice as long.
    Jim knew of that story. He also knew that terracing could help *his*
tribe. The problem was not only to convince his villagers; the problem
was time and money as well.
    Since most Chinantec cannot grow enough corn for themselves, they
must also work for the rich to earn money to buy more corn. Such

outside work doesn't leave a man enough time to develop new farming methods. Terracing would come with a price—the wages that a man would otherwise get working for someone else.

In 1973 with funds from his own pocket, Jim hired a group of workers to terrace a quarter acre of land. The mountain was so steep they could cut only three feet into the hillside with their shovels before hitting rock. Work was disappointingly slow until the men discovered that hoes worked better. Behind schedule, they planted a month later, and only *two* seeds into every hole.

Harvest proved to the Chinantec that it was the better way. The corn grew ten feet tall, and eight pounds of seed yielded more than four hundred pounds of corn. The next year a Christian fund provided money to pay more workers. A Rototiller arrived but broke down after only two terraces. Heavy rains packed the terraced soil to hard clay. The problems seemed to grow into insurmountable mountains.

Jim grew up on a dairy farm. He didn't know much about farming, but he knew how to figure out answers to a problem. He wasn't one to quit when things went hard.

When harvest time came, corn had grown ten feet tall again and on soil that had been abandoned by the villagers for being too poor to grow anything. The harvest yielded two tons of corn from two one-acre plots of land enriched by fertilizer and proper planting methods.

I walked with Jim along the terraces. "I am trying to improve their diet, too," he said to me. "I am trying crop rotation with wheat, oats, rice, cabbage, lima beans, and pole beans."

I saw some half eaten young cabbages in one place. "Jim," I said, "we kept the insects from our garden plots by growing lots of garlic and onions around the other stuff."

"I'll try that. I will try anything to help these people."

"Jim, is this field work slowing up your translation work?"

"On the contrary," he smiled his young enthusiastic grin. "I work alongside the men while they are terracing, and I learn their language faster. Furthermore, the Chinantec know by now for sure that I am interested in them as people. I overheard some of them say, 'He really loves us.' They also call me 'old man,' which is a term of respect."

"How old are you, 'old man'?" I laughed.

"I'm thirty-five," Jim replied, "and I pray and hope to have the translation done within a few more years. The Word of God is sown and beginning to take roots in these mountains. I am working with young men. I have a young translation assistant or informer, as we call them. These young men are so eager to share what they already know. It's not too much yet, but as they learn more from the Scriptures they tell me to pray for them. They say they wish to 'live straight and teach straight.' "

We trudged back to the plane. Jim pointed to a small hut in the distance. "This is our home," he said. We had had no time earlier to stop to see it. I didn't need to; I had seen others. I knew how these translators lived. They lived as the Indians did, in a simple mud hut, fighting rats, insects, mildew, prejudice, and poverty. They don't think they *are* anything special, I discovered, but they know they are *doing* something special.

As the little plane took off I looked over the many mountain ridges, and Jim pointed here and there. "Down there works another translator, and another over there. And where you see the brown spot, that's the beginning of another landing strip. They have worked on it for the last seven years, but the rains keep destroying it. As soon as we can land there, we can begin work among more tribes."

"How many *more* tribes need to be reached?" I asked quietly.

There was not a trace of a smile on this handsome, rugged young face when Jim answered, "Oh, there might be another two thousand tongues to go," he said soberly. "We seem to find more tribes nobody knew about as the work advances. From the human standpoint it could look hopeless to reach them all, but we serve an Almighty God!"

I nodded. Yes, it might look impossible to reach every tongue and tribe for Christ. But it will be done, and the tribes will be reached—one by one!

30
It's Up to the True American!

When the plane from Mexico City landed in Los Angeles, I had the same big lump of joy in my throat as I had had when we came back from the world tour.

Two young men, Tom and John, had gone and returned with me. The two brothers were brand-new Christians and bubbling over in their first love for Christ and His Church. This visit had been their introduction to mission work. They had traveled before in Europe, Africa, and any other place they ever wanted to visit, but until their recent conversion the two had been part of the typical affluent drinking and partying society. They also had been a great concern to their parents.

"I'll never be the same again," both said to me, and I knew what they meant. Nobody can leave the affluence of the American society and see how the rest of the world lives and be the same, unless one leaves his heart at home! Nobody can come back to America and not have a new appreciation of our great land, either.

Before John said goodbye, he looked at me with troubled eyes. "Hansi, I asked myself an honest question while I observed the translators and their hard work down there. Would *I* be willing to leave America and go to such places if that was God's will for my life? I am just not sure that I *could* do such a thing."

I looked into his open face and said slowly, "John, remember that you're only a babe in Christ. God doesn't demand the impossible of us. Should you ever be called to such a task, you'll mature first, and God will prepare you for it step by step."

I often think of a little story Corrie ten Boom loves to tell, and I related it to the boys. When she was just a little girl, she was afraid of future troubles, too. Her father sat at her bedside one night while she cried and said, "Corrie, when you and I go to Amsterdam, when do I give you your ticket—three weeks before?"

Corrie said, "No, you give it to me just before we get on the train."

Then Corrie's father said, "Exactly! And our wise Father in heaven knows when we're going to need things too."

"Don't run ahead of God and borrow trouble for tomorrow," I said. "God has every ticket for us ready whenever we need it. Live one day at a time with Him, grow in His grace, enjoy what God has given you in this beautiful land, and leave the future to Him."

I hoped my words had eased my young friends' minds as they were leaving. I hated to see them go—they were so refreshing to my spirit.

I need to remind myself often that my heavenly Father does hold things in His hands, and He does look after all of His children.

Since our return from the world tour I had gone through several spiritual crises. First, I had gotten busy as soon as I got home to find some simple wheelchairs for Madame Thieu. It proved more difficult than expected because simple wheelchairs are not available; the American manufacturers produce only very sophisticated kinds. We realized that the simple kind would have to be built. I set out to find the money for it—and for my Cambodian orphans.

Money for the orphans came in, but nothing came for the wheelchairs. That puzzled me. God had always provided for every need and emergency before. Why wasn't He opening the way for building wheelchairs?

We sent the money for my Jimmy and his ninety-six children to Thailand. From there it was several times hand-carried in, and the weeks crawled slowly by. Cambodia's situation seemed to deteriorate, and I waited impatiently for their rainy season to begin. I had not a doubt in my mind that God would spare Cambodia again. After all, the Gospel had to do its work for the many waiting hearts. God would never let anything happen that would stop His work from being finished.

When Cambodia fell, just days away from the beginning of the new monsoon, I was too stunned to accept it. Conflicting rumors flew around. I called anyone who might know something about it, but it was weeks before we got some facts. What we heard made us weep. I wasn't the only one who was so crushed by Cambodia's tragedy.

When I called "Daddy Jim," he told me that his organization had called all their office employees to a special day of fasting and prayer just before Phnom Penh fell. Their new children's hospital, built under unbelievable difficulties, had been ready to be opened just as the Khmer Rouge rolled in. The surgery instruments were laid out, the shelves filled with donated medicine, but the mission of mercy for the children of Cambodia had come too late.

Why, Lord, *why?*

The first two facts we knew for sure was that all the civilians had been forced to leave Phnom Penh and that they had saved the orphans of the Nutrition Center and taken them back to America on time.

What about my Jimmy and the Christian Angels Orphanage? Had they come out, too? Nobody seemed to know. I would awaken at night and see those little faces before me. Had they been driven out into the countryside to die? Would anybody feed them? Was Jimmy, the orphan director, with them, or had the Communists shot him?

As the word trickled hesitatingly from the American press that a bloodbath was taking place behind the now tightly closed bamboo curtain of Cambodia, my agony deepened.

"Why, Lord, why did it happen? Why did You give me those orphans just so that I would lose them again?"

I had many commitments to speak that I had to keep during that time. It became more and more difficult for me to make it through a message without tears. I couldn't get Jimmy and my orphans off my mind. Many an American audience wept with me when I asked them to pray for my orphans.

It was about three weeks later that I received a letter from my Jimmy. He had left Cambodia shortly before Phnom Penh fell, to see his mother in Korea. Maybe he realized that the end would be soon, and he wanted to give his mother the personal assurance of his conversion. He never had a question in his mind that he would return to his children and if needed, die with them.

Alas, Jimmy got as far as Thailand on his way back and couldn't go any further. No more planes could fly in; the Communists had the airport covered. Jimmy wrote that he went from place to place begging for one more plane to go in to get his children out. It was too late.

Seven of his orphans had come out on their own initiative, just days before. They had gone to one of Jimmy's friends, an American journalist, and asked where their "father" was.

The American was just packing to leave, and he told the orphans to come with him. He bought seven tickets to Bangkok for them, and they flew out in the nick of time. Jimmy and his seven children had a tearful reunion. Then the children were sent to Holland for adoption. What about the other eighty-nine who were left behind?

Cambodian refugees started to trickle across the borderline into Thailand. Jimmy went to a Christian broadcasting company that beamed messages into Cambodia, asking them to tell his Christian Angels orphans to come across the borderline into Thailand. Then he went up to the border to wait for them. They never came, but other orphans did, and thousands of refugees flooded across day after day.

Jimmy wrote us letter after letter, asking for help to assist them. We sent every dollar we could spare and some we couldn't. I also sent him the address of every church and of our personal friends I had met while in Bangkok.

It was then that I began to understand why God had kept us so long in Bangkok. As Jimmy went from address to address, my American friends rallied together to help the refugees. Such personal help was needed because some organizations didn't dare to do what had to be done. The Thai government threatened them with expulsion.

Jimmy wrote me in his letters that the Thai soldiers treated the Cambodian refugees very cruelly. Americans couldn't stay overnight near the border because the Khmer Rouge would come over the borderline at night, raiding and killing. Jimmy stayed in a refugee camp two kilometers away from Cambodia.

He wrote in his halting English, "Many people advise me not to stay nighttime there. But they don't know God stay with me and He guides me every step in His work. I do my best. Please pray for our orphans still in Cambodia. I miss them too much. When I meet them in my dreams, I am almost crazy. . . ."

I knew how he felt; I had the same problem. I asked God to let me find peace again, to help me to understand or to accept without it.

God did exactly that. A doctor friend who had heard me tell the story of my orphans and their all-night prayer meeting called for an all-night prayer meeting in someone's big office.

"If those kids can stay up all night praying, why can't *we* do the same?" he had said to me. "Let's try it!"

That night became a milestone in my Christian experience.

Several groups of people came and went; nobody was limited by set times. We had hours to reflect and search, we shared, we formed little circles to pray. By the early morning hours only a handful of young people and the doctor and I were left. We had again formed small groups to pray for each other. When it was time for me to give my request, I asked the group to pray for my peace of mind. I sobbed again as I told them about my Cambodian orphans.

The young people cried with me, and then one young woman said, "Hansi, God has given you your bleeding heart for a purpose. He is using it to rip our cold, unfeeling hearts wide open. We Americans need to find our compassion again. The news media have most of us convinced that we don't need to care anymore. I never thought about it until I listened to you that Cambodia is *people,* not a political pawn!"

But what about my orphans? Why couldn't we get them out? We did much praying that night, and when I left at dawn I had a new assurance in my heart. I knew my orphans were all right. They either were already with the Lord, or God would keep them in the hollow of His hand until He would return to take us all home. He could protect those kids from the sinister brainwashing of atheism and keep them to the end.

I wrote my Jimmy about it, and it comforted his troubled heart, too. He was so busy leading refugees to the Lord, handing out food, loving the children; he kept going day and night. It was his idea to print a cross on hundreds of children's T-shirts and under it print "Jesus Loves You." Jimmy would give suggestions, and my American friends would consider them and follow through. They all worked in harmony except for those who were afraid of the Thai authorities. Jimmy couldn't understand it. He was as simple as a child in his thinking. Why be afraid of the Thai government if God was on his side? Wasn't God stronger?

Yes, God is always stronger, and He used Jimmy to lead hundreds of refugees to Christ. By the time Jimmy had to leave Thailand because his visa had run out, more than seven hundred refugees had been baptized in the muddy river water into a new clean hope in Jesus Christ.

God gave Jimmy one of the greatest desires of his heart when we were able to fly him from Thailand into the United States to attend a Bible college in the Midwest. I will never forget when I welcomed him to America in person.

"I will do my best," he said to me. "Indochina needs more help. I will learn all I can, and God will give me a chance to work in His will. I want to do great things for my God!"

I wasn't so sure that God would be able to use Jimmy in Indochina by the time he had finished Bible college—but I didn't say anything. Why ask for the troubles of tomorrow? Why disturb his mind with my concerns? Although I wasn't sure any more that Jimmy would someday be a missionary to Indochina, I had come a long way in my thinking since I had seen him last in front of the Cambodian orphanage.

When Vietnam fell, I went through another time of emotional struggle. I finally understood why God had stopped our wheelchair project. There would have been no time to get them there before the Communists took over.

I would wake up at night and plead with God for my friends in South Vietnam. What would happen to Sut Thong? Would the Communists kill those precious people who had already suffered so much for their faith? What about the missionaries? We had no word about those in Cambodia or Vietnam.

As the weeks sped by into months, God let me find some answers that helped me greatly. One came to me when I met with Dr. Stanley, the international president of the child care organization Daddy Jim belonged to. Stanley was one of the last Americans to see Cambodia before it fell. He had shared the Lord's Supper with a group of Cambodians and had encouraged them to be true to God. He had also pleaded with Vaughn to come and join his young wife and three little children who were leaving Cambodia with the orphan transport. Vaughn refused to leave. "I have my parents and all my brothers and sisters here. They do not know the Lord; I must stay with them!"

Dr. Stanley talked to Vaughn over wireless radio from Bangkok just hours before the city fell. Vaughn sobbed into the speaker with joy. *"All* my family has accepted the Lord except my father. Pray for him."

The last word we had from Vaughn came in a letter that was smuggled out by someone who had been permitted to leave the French embassy and had come out on a lone convoy into Thailand. The note said that the Khmer Rouge forced everyone to leave the safety of the embassy. Vaughn would now try to walk the many miles to the Thai border. Nobody has heard from him since.

Dr. Stanley and I cried together as he told me about Vaughn's lonely little wife. The three children seemed to enjoy America.

"Hansi," Dr. Stanley said, "I have asked God so many times *why* it all had to happen. The latest word we have from Cambodian refugees seems to give me great comfort. I couldn't understand *why*, for instance, the civilians of Phnom Penh had to be driven out into the rains of the jungle country. We knew that an estimated 3½ million would die of hunger and exposure.

"I know it wasn't God's will that it happened, but God made a modern Acts of the Apostle story out of all the horror. As our new believers from Phnom Penh were spreading all over the country, they preached Christ in every place we hadn't been able to go. Thousands of people had to die, but they died with a new hope. We have enough evidence to believe that Cambodia's revival is not over yet but is spreading and growing even now."

I told Dr. Stanley what God had said to me when I stood on the steps of that Cambodian hospital. He nodded. "I believe it more from day to day. It's happening everywhere. God *will* finish His work even through the wrath of men."

I met with several of the missionaries who came back to America after they had to leave Indochina. I heard from them what happened in those last days.

Eugene and his family were forced to leave by the embassy; so were the girls of the Nutrition Center. Sandra almost didn't get permission to take her Simon. The girls prayed around the clock, and Simon's leave was okayed.

The American ambassador in Cambodia smiled when he saw those people off. "Don't worry," he said, "you'll be back in a few weeks!"

Eugene slipped back into Phnom Penh even after the embassy pulled out and almost didn't make it. He stayed with his "babes in Christ" to the last moment. He and every one of our missionaries died a thousand deaths when they had to leave.

I thought of John in the Central Highlands and what he had said to me. Sau, the tribal chief, blessed his two sons and told them to leave for America. "They are *your* sons," he told John and Jo. Sau and Kar could have fled, too. They stayed behind with their people. The last word we have had is that Sau is in a Communist prison.

I saw Don and Paul again. "Don," I said, "I was afraid you had stayed too long in Saigon. We prayed for all of you day and night."

"We could tell," Don smiled his contagious smile. "We had a few close calls."

Paul smiled his shy smile when I said, "I thought of you too, and your three months' food supply for your streetboys. Did it last?"

"We had just enough," Paul said, "and nothing left for the Communists to take away from our boys!"

Madame Le called me one day. We had searched for her in Guam and other places with no trace of her. When she called, she had practically become my neighbor. She, eleven children of hers, and other relatives live now in a big house near us in a beach town.

"I prayed one night," she said, "for I needed advice. I found your card in my purse!" It was a miracle that she had made it.

"I had smuggled my twelve children away on the boat," she told me. "I wanted to stay and die with my people. The government troops found the boat and brought my family back and put them into prison. I paid much to get them out; I wanted to send them again but they refused to go without me. They said, 'Mother, we either go together or we stay and die together.' So I came with them. One daughter stayed behind. She had a baby and was too weak. I cry much for her."

I looked at that little woman. She and her family work long hours for minimum wages in a California factory that makes sandals. "Madame Le," I said to her, "I told you I would pray that you would not die with your people. My God has answered my prayers. You are alive—and God has a purpose for your life here in America."

"I know," she said. "I knew that you prayed. I could feel it. Keep praying for us, we need it. It is hard for us to learn so much in this new land."

I'll never forget when I saw General Khang and his little wife again. He had gotten all of his twenty-one family members out: parents, brothers, sisters, and his in-laws. Bill and Virginia had sponsored all of them and when the group arrived, one of the churches had rallied together to back the old couple up. Bill and Virginia had neither the room nor the money to take care of all of them, but when a whole church stepped in, things began to move. Houses were made available, furniture and linen brought in, and one local businessman set up an account at the grocery store where the Vietnamese refugees could buy their food and charge it to him.

General Khang looked at me and smiled. "Hansi," he said, "the American people are very generous, but the press is funny. I am supposedly one of those *high* government officials who came to America with many gold bars. Too bad it isn't true. I came out last, after my family was smuggled out by Don, and I escaped in my pants and shirt, not even in a jacket."

"General Khang," I interrupted him, "the American press isn't funny; they have been deliberately vicious, and I have a hard time believing what I am seeing in our land at the present time."

I paused and remembered what Daddy Jim had said to me over the telephone shortly after Vietnam fell. Poor Daddy Jim! I pictured him pacing the floor of his office like a caged lion when the news media would downgrade anything about Cambodia and South Vietnam and tolerate, even excuse, *any* move the Communists made. A local newspaper editor called him right after the fall of Saigon and said, "Jim, you are probably the best expert on Indochina this city has. What reasons would you give that America lost Cambodia and Vietnam?"

"I hate to answer that to *you*," Jim replied grimly. "I blame the American news media entirely for it. They decided to drop these two lands, and they caused the defeat!"

I didn't share these thoughts with the general, but changed the subject.

"General Khang, how do you like it in America?"

"Hansi, I have liked America for a long time. I visited here often in the years before. I have friends in the Pentagon. I want to believe that I don't have to stay in the United States all my life. I am Vietnamese and I hope that someday I can return to a free Vietnam."

I looked at him and ached. How well I remembered my first year in America. All I could think of was my great desire to go back home someday. I knew things would look better for the Vietnamese refugees in years to come. They would melt into the great American melting pot as all of us had and feel more at home.

"Sir," I said, "I have one more question. What do you see for America's future?"

General Khang looked almost grim when he answered me. "Hansi," he tried to keep his voice steady, "when the American helicopter carried the ambassador and me out of Saigon, I looked down at the city and I thought, 'I am dreaming a terrible dream. It is *not* true. It cannot be true. My homeland is *not* becoming another Communist land. We fought too long and too hard for our freedom to lose it now.' "

Mrs. Khang wiped her tears. The general continued, "Hansi, nobody thinks that it *really can* happen to them. The American people are thinking the same way. They think what happened to other lands could not happen to America. Let me tell you, it *can* happen to America, too!"

"Do you think it will happen?" I asked and held my breath.

"I do not know," my Vietnamese friend said. "I have studied American history for years—Americans are a unique people. They go along and act very unconcerned, but if a national crisis arises they stand up, unite, and fight. I hope they will do it again in the future!"

"But what if they stand up and fight when it is too late?" I asked.

"Then I shall pity this nation as I have never pitied anyone before, including my own people," said the general. "If the Americans lose their freedom, nobody else will have ever suffered more than they will. Nobody ever had as much to lose as they have. So far, they still have the liberty to decide for themselves where America will go. For now it is still up to the American people."

I nodded, "It's up to the *true* Americans, I believe. May God wake us all up before it is too late. May we see and act—*now!*"

Because this book is a tribute to *every* true American, *every* Christian denomination and *every* American service organization, I have avoided surnames, special names and labels.

If anyone wants more detailed information, it can be obtained by writing to the author at P.O. Box 2110, Orange, CA 92669.